No-Fight Divorce

No-Fight Divorce

Spend Less Money, Save Time, and Avoid Conflict Using Mediation

BRETTE MCWHORTER SEMBER, J.D.

McGraw·Hill

New York Chicago San Francisco Lisbon London Madrid Mexico City
Milan New Delhi San Juan Seoul Singapore Sydney Toronto

The McGraw·Hill Companies

Library of Congress Cataloging-in-Publication Data

Sember, Brette McWhorter, 1968–
    No-fight divorce: spend less money, save time, and avoid conflict using mediation /
Brette McWhorter Sember.
        p.   cm.
     ISBN 0-07-145613-9 (book : alk. paper)
     1. Divorce mediation—United States.   I. Title.

   KF535.Z9S465   2005
   346.7301'66—dc22   2005004862

1 2 3 4 5 6 7 8 9 0   FGR/FGR   0 9 8 7 6 5

ISBN 0-07-145613-9

McGraw-Hill books are available at special quantity discounts to use as premiums and sales
promotions, or for use in corporate training programs. For more information, please write to the
Director of Special Sales, Professional Publishing, McGraw-Hill, Two Penn Plaza, New York, NY
10121-2298. Or contact your local bookstore.

The information in this book is designed to give you a broad overview of the current state of the
law about topics in the book and is provided for basic information purposes only. Laws differ in
each state and are constantly evolving and changing and no book can be completely up to date
and accurate. It is important to consult with an attorney and mediator in your state to
understand the laws that apply to you and obtain personal advice. This book is not a substitute
for legal or mediation advice.

This book is printed on acid-free paper.

Contents

9 Bumps in the Road: Solving Mediation Problems   127

10 Closing the Book: Finalizing Your Divorce   143

Introduction

Maria and Bo had been married for fifteen years and had two children. When they decided to get a divorce, they consulted attorneys, and Maria's attorney suggested mediation. Neither of them had heard of mediation before. They interviewed a few mediators and found one they liked. They went to mediation once a week for eight weeks and worked out a complete settlement agreement for their divorce. They agreed that they would share custody of their children, each spending half the time with the kids, something Bo's attorney said would probably never have been considered by a judge if the case had gone to court.

Mediation is a choice that will work for almost every couple. It encourages compromise, consideration, real thought, flexibility, healing, and creative solutions. Mediation allows the two of you to take control of your situation and make the decisions about how you're going to end your marriage. When you mediate, you work with a professional mediator who helps you decide all of the issues in your divorce yourselves. There's no judge telling you what to do, no outrageous attorney bills, and no loss of control. You can treat each other civilly and not feel as if you're on two different sides.

How much do you really know about mediation? To find out, indicate whether the following statements are true or false:

_____ 1. Mediation costs more than if we just go to court for our divorce.

_____ 2. To mediate, we have to know what kind of settlement we want.

_____ 3. Mediators are hard to find.

_____ 4. Mediation takes longer than if we just go to court for our divorce.

_____ 5. Mediation is like some kind of therapy and is all about feelings and relationships.

_____ 6. If we don't agree about big things like custody or property settlements, mediation is a waste of our time.

_____ 7. If we start to mediate our divorce but decide it doesn't work and have to go to court, we've hurt our case.

_____ 8. Mediation is often unfair to women, since men usually take charge and demand what they want and women are bullied into giving in.

_____ 9. When we mediate, we essentially give up all of our rights.

_____ 10. If we argue and fight a lot, mediation is not a good choice.

_____ 11. It's really best to leave divorce to the professionals and let them handle it for us.

The answers to all of these are false. Mediation is less expensive and less time consuming than traditional divorce. The purpose of mediation is to help you create a settlement—you don't have to know what you want when you walk in the door. There are mediators in every state and every city in the United States. Just look in the phone book or consult Appendix B of this book.

Mediation is not therapy but is a decision-making process that takes into consideration both parties' wants and needs. In mediation you always have the right to go to court, and none of your legal rights are affected. Mediation is a chance for you and your spouse to make decisions together, away from the gladiator ring that is divorce court.

Both men and women benefit from mediation, and no one is at a disadvantage. Each has the opportunity to speak and present suggestions, and each must listen to the other and come to a mutually agreeable decision. The mediator is there to make sure you each have equal time and completely understand everything you are agreeing to. Mediation works for couples who are deeply conflicted as well as those who are more agreeable. It is a good solution for most divorces because you are the ones who understand your situation the best, and therefore, you are the ones best equipped to make decisions about it.

Divorcing is one of the most difficult things you will ever do in your life. It is painful, frustrating, frightening, and completely life altering to end a marriage. Why make it more difficult than it has to be? Traditional divorce takes a bad situation and just makes it worse. Consider the path of a typical court divorce:

Joel and Rita's marriage was in turmoil for years before they finally decided to divorce. They thought that making the decision to divorce was going to be the hard part. It took many arguments, hurt feelings, sleepless nights, and therapy sessions before they decided their marriage wasn't going to work. Actually getting the divorce had to be easier, they thought. They were wrong.

Rita hired a lawyer who told her he could take charge of the situation and get her everything she wanted in the divorce. Because she was scared and uncertain of how it all worked, she agreed. The lawyer immediately filed papers and had Joel served at work. The papers sought an emergency court order to have him removed from the home and to grant temporary custody of their children to Rita, along with temporary child support and alimony. Being served with divorce papers at work absolutely enraged Joel, and when he read them he could not believe how unreasonable it all was. He felt betrayed and angry.

Joel hired his own lawyer, who made demands very similar to those made by Rita's lawyer. Joel and Rita had to go in for a short hearing to decide the temporary orders (preliminary orders by the court about temporary things like custody and alimony while the case is ongoing). There were witnesses who testified about custody and financial matters.

Once the temporary orders were in place, the rest of the case moved forward. The lawyers subpoenaed all kinds of paperwork, sent interrogatories, arranged depositions, and often didn't have time to return Joel's or Rita's phone calls. Joel and Rita were asked time and again to repeat the negative things about each other and find reasons why the other person should not get what he or she wanted. They spent all their time magnifying each other's mistakes and faults, and their dislike and distrust of each other grew. After months and months, the case was finally scheduled for trial. By the time of the trial, Joel and Rita were convinced they were complete enemies and were having a very difficult time parenting their children together. The kids were having trouble in school, and the oldest child was threatening to go live with a grandparent.

Joel and Rita went to trial, and their attorneys argued persuasively for their positions. They each testified and had many witnesses. Both of them cried on the witness stand. After a full week, the trial ended, but then they had to wait to get the judge's decision in the mail. When it came, neither one of them was happy with the result. And neither one of them knew how to deal with the sense of letdown they felt when it was over. They were fully charged and ready for battle for a year while the divorce was pending, and then suddenly it was all over and they had no closure or ending to it all. It took them a while to adjust to the fact that they now had to arrange their lives around this piece of paper, which told them when they could see their kids and how they were going to divide up their money.

Joel and Rita were angry at each other, at their lawyers, and at the judge. They returned to court several times in the ensuing years, arguing over changes in custody or increases in child support. They never really recovered from the divorce and hated each other for years afterward. They couldn't even sit together at their daughter's graduation.

This is unfortunately the path a typical divorce takes. Even if a case settles before it gets to trial, the parties are still already trained to think of and treat each other negatively. Judges often have to issue boilerplate judgments simply because they do not have time or enough detailed information to craft a personal plan for each family. Many people find it difficult to live their lives according to a judgment that is not tailored to their lives.

Mediation uses a completely different model. In mediation you are encouraged to approach your divorce cooperatively. Obviously, you're not on the same wavelength about a lot of things, and there are probably many things you disagree about, but mediation is designed to help you work through those problems to come up with solutions that will work for both of you, as well as your children, if you have any.

To find out if mediation is something you should consider, indicate whether the following statements are true or false for your situation:

___ 1. I want to get my divorce over with as quickly as possible.
___ 2. I want to spend as little money as I can, while still getting a good outcome for my divorce.
___ 3. I want our children to come through this with as few scratches as possible.
___ 4. I want to walk away from this divorce equipped to live my own independent life.
___ 5. I may not love my spouse anymore, but I don't need to tar and feather him or her (at least most days).

If you answered true to any of these, then mediation is a choice you should consider.

You might still be hesitating about mediation because you feel scared, uncertain, nervous, confused, hurt, angry, vindictive, or overwhelmed. What you are feeling is a normal reaction to divorce.

You can get through this time in your life, and there is a good chance that mediation can help you do it.

This book is designed to be a source of information and help as you mediate your divorce, by explaining every step along the way and offering real and practical suggestions to make mediation go more smoothly and be more effective. I practiced family and matrimonial law and was truly dissatisfied with the way the system worked. As a law guardian for children in these cases, I saw firsthand how destructive the litigation process was for families. I jumped at the chance to learn to mediate and found that mediation offered families a better and more civilized, reasonable, and delicate process that was about finding solutions instead of creating problems. I saw the difference mediation made in the lives of my clients, and I know it can make a difference in your life, too.

I hope that this book can help you understand what mediation is, how it works, and how to get the most out of it. This book has been written for any kind of couple and offers information that applies to all types of committed partnerships. Whether you are married, are unmarried and living together, have children, or are only beginning to consider ending your relationship, let this book be your guide.

Because mediation is a process that involves communication, this book emphasizes the communication skills you need to get the most out of it. In the chapters you will find special sections called "Words That Work"—real things you can say to your spouse, your mediator, or other people involved in your mediation, to communicate problems, find solutions, or express yourself. Sometimes people who feel as if they aren't good talkers worry that they will not succeed in mediation. This is not true at all. Your mediator is there to help you express yourself, and this book provides you with many useful tools and ways to effectively put words to use.

Because each state varies in its divorce laws and procedures and because the laws are ever changing, it is important that you talk with an attorney in your state to learn the details about your state's laws. The information in this book provides an overview of divorce law and how mediation works, but mediators can differ in their approaches. This book has been written from the perspective of my approach to mediation, an approach that I hope you will find as stress reducing, time saving, financially sensible, and emotionally healthy as I have found it to be in my professional experiences.

I hope you give mediation a try. I truly believe it is the most reasonable way to end a marriage and know that the couples I mediated with found it to be an excellent solution.

◄ 1 ►

Nuts and Bolts

Understanding Why Mediation Works

Lara and Declan went to mediation because her sister had used it successfully. After it was over, Declan felt that it had worked well for them. When they first decided to get divorced, he felt very out of control—as if his entire life were suddenly up for grabs. But mediation made him feel he had taken control back and was in charge of his own life. Lara and Declan used mediation to divide their property and debts, to decide about alimony, and to determine who would file for divorce and what legal reason for divorce they would use. The mediator helped Lara and Declan find compromises that worked for both of them, such as subletting their apartment to earn more than their rent and then each renting a smaller apartment themselves. Declan knew this was something he never would have thought of.

• • •

Mediation is a flexible and creative process that encourages finding solutions that both you and your spouse can live with. Before you can decide if mediation is a viable option for your situation, it's important to get a clear picture of what exactly mediation is. Some people picture mediation as a formal legal process with the mediator listening to both sides and then making a decision, but interestingly enough, mediation doesn't work that way.

Where Mediation Came From

Mediation is a type of alternative dispute resolution (a problem-solving method) that was first used in divorce and family law in the 1970s when attorneys and other divorce professionals became dissatisfied with the process. (This was also around the time when more and more people were getting divorced; skyrocketing divorce rates created a great demand for services.) They were frustrated that divorce had to always be about conflict. There was no cooperative element, and spouses were pitted against each other as if they were in a war. It seemed incongruous that people who had once lived together and raised a family were suddenly encouraged not to speak to each other and act as if all they wanted to do was win. The founders of the divorce mediation movement believed that there were better, more therapeutic ways to end marriages than the traditional adversarial process.

The Basics of Mediation

Mediation is a process in which two spouses work together with a neutral third-party mediator to reach decisions about the issues involved in their divorce. Mediation is also often used in other family law cases—such as custody disputes, child support cases, or visitation problems—between couples who are already divorced or who were never married.

- **Mediation gives the control back to the couple.** Throughout your marriage you made decisions together about how you were going to live your lives, raise your children, and manage your money. Just because you're getting divorced does not mean you should simply hand over all of those decisions to someone else.

Mediation allows you to make decisions together that will affect the rest of your lives. When you allow a judge to decide your case, he or she never truly gets to know you. The judge never talks to you alone and gets to know your feelings. In fact, the judge might never even hear you say a single word! Judges decide divorces according to set rules and standards, based only on the evidence that is presented in court. They don't have time to make each decision personal and tailored to the couple's needs. But when you use mediation, you can personalize your divorce agreement and incorporate everything that is important to you. You and your spouse make choices that are suited to your specific situation, which you both agree to.

- **Mediation is about compromise.** Many people think that divorce has to be an all-out war. The way we often talk about divorce is very confrontational: "take him to the cleaners," "win custody," and so on. Divorce doesn't have to be about conflict, winning, losing, or punishing the other person. Mediation approaches the divorce process with compromise in mind. You and your spouse each have outcomes you would like, and often these are very compatible with each other. When you don't agree, mediation helps you find a way to compromise enough so that you both walk away believing that you've reached a fair and livable decision.

- **Mediation is about problem solving.** There are an array of decisions to make when you get divorced, and many are not easy. The mediator helps you think in a logical and orderly way about the problems confronting you, helps you understand the decisions you need to make (many of which are not obvious to you at the beginning), and helps you discover and create solutions that are tailored to your specific issues. When an issue is resolved in mediation, it is not about one person getting what he or she wants and the other person losing. There are no losers in mediation.

- **Mediation emphasizes self-determination.** You and your spouse have the power to make decisions about your own situation. To make decisions you must become empowered with knowledge. The mediation process helps the parties become knowledgeable about the law, their situation, the other person's position, and all

3

the options available. Mediation opens your eyes to possibilities you might not have considered and gives you the power to decide what you want to do.

• **Mediation is flexible.** Mediation is designed to allow you and your spouse to choose solutions that are carefully crafted to meet all of your family's needs. Cookie-cutter solutions, often found in traditional divorce court, are not imposed upon you.

• **Mediation has no time limits.** In most cases, unless you're in court-ordered mediation, you can take as long as you need to decide things. You have time to think and talk through the issues. When you go to court, there is often a rigid time frame in which your case must be decided. Mediation gives you the freedom to think things through and see how they develop. Sometimes you just can't know if a solution or an arrangement is going to work until you've actually tried it. In mediation you have time to do that.

How Mediation Works

When you decide to mediate, you and your spouse will meet with a mediator for approximately six to ten sessions, each session lasting between one and two hours. You can create a schedule that suits you and your spouse and meet for as many sessions as you need, although many mediators recommend meeting once a week if possible so that you can keep the ball rolling.

The mediator guides you through all the decisions you must make in your case and explains how your decisions will become part of your divorce agreement. Your mediator is your guide, not a decision maker, who suggests options and helps you analyze situations and problems. He or she also provides legal information to help you understand the laws and the choices available to you, often encouraging you to devise creative solutions that you and your spouse can live with.

Mediation has a cooperative atmosphere, not a confrontational one. You and your spouse talk through issues and look for solutions that you can both be comfortable with. This doesn't mean you kiss and make up, but you are encouraged to listen to each other's point of view and to strive to work together. Each of you is encouraged to talk and suggest possible solutions, and each of you is expected to listen to the other person's ideas.

You and your spouse will need to retain separate attorneys to represent each of you. These attorneys do not come to the mediation sessions (unless you ask them to), nor do they speak to your spouse's attorney. Your attorney explains your state's divorce laws, what requirements you must meet (having to do with such things as residency, papers to be filed, child support laws, and court appearances), and what choices you have (concerning such issues as the grounds or reasons available for divorce, different ways to file for divorce, and custody arrangement options). Your attorney is a source of information for you and is also a good sounding board. He or she will advise you as to how strong your case would be if you chose to go to court and let a judge decide. This can help you understand what your alternatives are if you decide not to complete mediation. Your attorney will also review your final mediated divorce agreement, and one of the attorneys will file court papers in order to finalize the divorce.

What Mediation Resolves

Mediation can be used in any kind of dispute or disagreement, although in this book we will talk about its use in divorce or family law cases. When you mediate your divorce, you resolve all the legal issues involved in your case: custody, visitation, how to divide attorney and mediator fees, what legal path you will follow to finalize your divorce, property settlement, alimony, and child support. When you complete mediation, you will have a written agreement that sets out all of the decisions you have made. This document then either will be submitted to the court as it is written by your mediator or will be rewritten by your attorney into a specific format required in your state and submitted to the court.

In mediation you also resolve issues that are not usually part of a court judgment. Mediation gives you the freedom to work out small issues that often are the stumbling points for many couples but are not normally decided by a court. For example, you can reach agreements about how you will treat each other, when you will introduce your children to new partners, or what kind of contact you will have with each other's friends.

Mediation is also important because it helps you resolve the four parts of a divorce:

- The **legal divorce** is granted by the court and divides all of your assets and debts—it deals with the business end of your divorce.
- The **social divorce** defines the changes in your lifestyle and friendships because of the divorce.
- The **emotional divorce** affects your feelings as you cope with the divorce.
- The **physical divorce** is the literal separation of your belongings and yourselves.

While a traditional divorce only handles the legal end of divorce, mediation is sensitive to all four of these aspects and helps you work out plans for handling all of them.

Additionally, mediation helps you resolve and reorganize the three partnerships that you and your spouse may have: the financial partnership, the emotional partnership, and the parenting partnership. When you mediate, you work out solutions for dissolving your financial partnership, including dividing up your assets and debts and thinking about child support and alimony. You also come to grips with the end of your emotional partnership and attain closure for this relationship. Mediation allows you to find a way to continue your parenting partnership, by creating a parenting plan that allows both of you to continue raising your children together.

Who Are Mediators?

Mediators are trained professionals who guide you through the decisions facing you. Mediators are often attorneys or therapists and should have specific training and experience in divorce mediation. For more information about mediators, see Chapter 3.

What Mediation Costs

Mediators normally require a retainer (or up-front) fee, which is applied against work done out of sessions and from which the fees for the first few sessions may also be deducted. Once the retainer fee is used up, you are billed hourly for the mediation sessions and only pay for the time you actually use. Mediation rates vary across the country but range between $75 and $200 an hour, depending on the mediator's experience and qualifications.

Even though you will be retaining an attorney and a mediator, the cost of a mediated divorce ends up being much less than a traditional one. Average total costs of mediation range from $3,000 to $5,000, whereas the average litigated divorce costs about $10,000 on average. It simply takes many more hours to have an attorney litigate your case than to have a mediator mediate your case, and litigating attorneys usually charge a higher hourly rate than mediators. Even though most divorce cases do settle before they go to trial, attorneys must prepare for trial in case it does happen. In fact, most settlements come on the eve of a trial, when all the trial preparation has already been done (and charged to your account).

Important Aspects of Mediation

Mediation has three important components, which make it a process that is fair and user-friendly.

Neutrality

Your mediator will remain completely neutral throughout the entire process and will act as your guide and resource. He or she won't take either person's side or try to convince either one of you of anything. He or she will act and appear completely impartial and unbiased, without having any particular stake in any outcome. It is important that both parties believe the mediator is neutral, because if there are any lingering doubts, it will be difficult for both of you to trust the mediator and listen openly to his or her suggestions.

Some mediators refuse to meet separately with either party because it can make the other spouse feel suspicious. Other mediators have no problem doing this but set clear ground rules. You might agree that everything you discuss in private with the mediator remains private and is not shared with the other spouse, or you might agree that anything that is discussed is information that can be shared with the other spouse.

Confidentiality

Everything you discuss with your mediator is in confidence, and he or she can't discuss it with anyone. Your sessions are completely private. However, it's important to understand that your mediator is not acting as a therapist or an attorney, and he or she could be subpoenaed to testify in court about things discussed during mediation. This is a very rare occurrence, though. Outside of that, your mediator will keep your information completely private.

Financial Disclosure

One of the most important parts of mediation is complete financial disclosure. When your divorce is handled in court, you and your spouse are required to provide each other with complete information about your financial situations, including income, debts, investments, bank accounts, property, and so on. If you fail to provide complete disclosure, you can be held in contempt of court.

In mediation both parties must provide complete financial disclosure, just as in court. Mediation cannot work if one person withholds information. It is essential that all the facts are laid out on the table for both of you to see so that you can negotiate fairly and honestly and not have to worry that there is anything hidden.

In some states you must sign a sworn statement that you have provided complete financial disclosure during mediation; this is then filed as part of your divorce. If your state does not require this, your mediator should require both of you to sign a notarized document stating this. Chapter 8 contains more information about financial disclosure.

Long-Term Effects

One of the biggest benefits of mediation is its long-term effects. Litigated divorce can leave a bad taste in your mouth, so to speak. You and your spouse end your marriage with conflict. You go on record, saying damaging and hurtful things about each other, and in fact, you are encouraged to think of as many bad things as you can about your spouse. You end up with a court decision that doesn't give either one of you what you want, and you part as enemies.

When you meditate your divorce, you and your spouse work cooperatively to end your marriage, and you part on reasonable terms. You end up with an agreement that works for both of you and for your children, and there is not as much resentment and anger.

Mediation teaches you how to solve future disputes that may come up so you don't need to return to court. Many couples or families that litigate divorces end up in a revolving door to the courtroom. They get one thing resolved, and then situations change or other problems arise and, because they have not learned how to resolve problems on their own, they spin right back around through the door into the courtroom again. This is not only frustrating but also damaging for the children in the family, and it encourages an atmosphere of hostility and negativity.

Attorneys and judges who work in family and divorce court know these families have no conflict-resolution skills. They are helpless in the face of any kind of disagreement or problem and always turn around and file more papers, spend more money on

Is Mediation a Good Option for You?

Litigated Divorce

Takes six months to two years to complete.

Costs about $10,000 on average.

Often requires one person to legally blame the other for the end of the marriage.

Requires you to testify in court and say bad things about each other.

Involves a judge who does not get to know you, your children, or your individual situation.

Lawyers speak for you.

Requires you to fit into preconceived notions or standards.

Events and appearances happen according to the judge's and lawyers' schedules.

Involves lots of complicated paperwork.

Does not consider nontraditional situations or provide solutions in those instances.

Mediated Divorce

Takes several months to complete.

Costs about $4,000 on average.

Acknowledges that ending the marriage is a mutual decision with no blame attached.

Requires no testimony or court appearances.

Involves a mediator who gets to know you and your children and helps you make decisions that work best for all of you.

Enables you to speak for yourself and communicate everything you think is important.

Allows you to set your own standards and do what feels right to the two of you.

Lets you get things done when you want to.

Involves very little paperwork.

Welcomes couples who are unmarried partners, whether gay or heterosexual, and allows these families to find solutions to their problems.

Litigation	Mediation
Discourages you from talking to each other about issues in the case.	Encourages you to talk to each other to try to resolve things.
Assumes you and your spouse are enemies.	Assumes you and your spouse have a common goal and an ongoing relationship as parents.
Judges your parenting abilities and decides that one parent is better than the other.	Encourages you to continue to trust and rely on each other as parents.
Often involves very little face-to-face, in-person contact with your lawyer.	Is all about personal, face-to-face contact with your mediator.
Often focuses on negative information.	Focuses on positive things and highlights your agreements.
Has a very high appeals rate. In many states, more than half of the litigated cases are appealed.	Has a very low appeals rate because both parties came up with and agreed to everything in the divorce judgment.
Is all about moving people through the system.	Is all about compassion for your situation and helping you make decisions for yourselves at your own rate.
Expects people to behave in an unreasonable manner.	Expects people to behave in a reasonable, civil, honest way.
Does nothing to help you resolve the personal side of divorce.	Allows you to find closure and talk about your feelings.
Is a public process that takes place in public. All documents filed are public record.	Is a private process that happens in a private place with a mediator you personally select. Nothing is public record other than the final settlement you file with the court and other required court forms.

attorneys, and take up more of the judicial system's resources. Couples who mediate rarely need to return to the judicial system and learn to solve problems together.

Mediation also benefits children. Parents learn that even though they may no longer be partners, they can still be parents together. When there are children involved, mediation creates a parenting plan (also known as custody and visitation), which devises a family arrangement that maximizes each parent's time with the children. Parents are not fighting over ownership of their children. Instead, they think and talk about how they can best continue to parent together and what kind of arrangement they can create that will be best for the children. Children are not pawns or objects of strategy, and in mediation they are not treated as such. Children see that their parents still respect each other and believe they are a family. They don't feel as if they must choose sides, because there are no sides. The emphasis is on finding a solution that will work for everyone in the family, instead of pursuing what you want without regard to the needs of the family. Children of parents who mediate experience less stress during the process than children of parents who litigate. These children whose parents mediate also learn that the best way to resolve a conflict is through compromise and reasonable discussion, instead of argument and underhanded tactics.

How Mediation Differs from Other Alternative Dispute-Resolution Processes

Mediation shares some similarities with other methods of dispute resolution, but it is not the same.

Arbitration

Many people confuse mediation with arbitration. Arbitration, like mediation, is an out-of-court dispute-resolution method, but the difference is that arbitration is not a cooperative process. In arbitration a decision maker listens to the arguments and points of view from both sides and then reaches a decision about how the matter should be resolved. The arbitrator makes the decision, not the parties involved. While arbitration can be informal and less intimidating than a courtroom proceeding, all the decision-making power is in the hands of the arbitrator, not the parties.

Formal binding arbitration is not an option for divorce, but in some states there are nonbinding arbitration programs for divorce, which are used as part of the settlement process. In these programs the attorney for each side presents his or her position to an experienced matrimonial attorney who acts as the arbitrator. The arbitrator then tells the parties how he or she thinks a judge would decide the case, but this is only a recommendation and does not have to be followed. This then gives the parties a good look at what a judge's decision might be and allows them to try to negotiate a settlement so that they can avoid having a trial. This method works well in traditional divorce cases where there is no settlement in sight and a trial would be lengthy and expensive.

Collaborative Law

Collaborative law is a new, growing field in which each party hires a collaborative lawyer. The collaborative attorneys work together to try to reach an agreement. These attorneys will only work on settlements and will not handle litigated cases. Your collaborative attorneys meet with each other and may also meet with you or your spouse present. Their goal is to find a mutually agreeable solution and to avoid litigation. If a settlement is not reached, these attorneys will not take the case to court, and you will need to locate new trial attorneys.

Collaborative law works well for couples who are not comfortable negotiating for themselves and would prefer to have an attorney handle the negotiations. The downside is that you and your spouse cannot negotiate directly. It may take longer to reach a settlement, since the attorneys must discuss settlement options, go back to check with their clients, and then discuss settlement options again. This cycle repeats if clients don't agree. It also can be more expensive than mediation. Instead of paying one mediator, you and your spouse each pay your own attorney (who charges higher rates than mediators do) to negotiate the settlement for you.

When you use collaborative law, it is important that you select an attorney who understands you and what you want out of the settlement. He or she is going to be speaking for you and negotiating on your behalf, so it's important that he or she have a clear understanding of what you want and will agree to.

Types of Mediation

The most common type is traditional mediation, which involves one mediator working with the two of you at your request. There are some other types, though.

Court-Ordered Mediation

If you are attending mediation because the court required you to, you may feel resentful. It's not easy to have to do everything a judge decides you should do. However, if you can embrace mediation as a way to make your own decisions and take charge of your situation, you will soon realize that it can help you find solutions more easily than a judge can. The problem with court-ordered mediation is that mediation is supposed to be a voluntary process, but despite the fact that you're compelled to attend court-ordered mediation, many of the couples who come to court-ordered mediation do end up negotiating settlements in mediation.

There are two types of court-ordered mediation. The nonreporting type just requires you to try the mediation process, and nothing is sent to the court if you are not able to reach a settlement. The reporting type requires the mediator to send a report to the judge if you do not reach an agreement. This report can point out who was cooperative and who was not, what your major points of disagreement are, what a good solution would be, and what your positions are.

In nonreporting mediation you can feel free to honestly try to work toward a solution. Florida, for example, has enacted a law requiring mediators who handle court-ordered cases to protect their clients' confidentiality (and not disclose information, even to the court). In reporting mediation, though, you should be careful about what you say and do, since if you do not settle, it will all be shared with the judge. Talk to your attorney about what you should and should not share in reporting mediation.

Suggestions for Successful Court-Ordered Mediation
- Find out if the mediator reports back to the court or not.
- Approach it with good intentions, and try to reach a settlement in good faith.
- Be aware that this type of mediation is even further away from therapy than regular mediation is. You have very little time and may have no guarantee of complete confidentiality, so you have to focus just on the legal issues at hand and finding a legal solution for them.
- Get clear advice from your attorney about how the mediation could affect your case, what you should not discuss, and what kind of settlement would be a reasonable one in your case.
- Don't miss sessions, since this can make you look bad to the judge.

Co-Mediation

Co-mediation occurs when two mediators work together with a couple. This approach can be very effective in certain situations. For example, if a heterosexual couple hires a man and a woman to co-mediate, both members of the couple may feel that they are understood, that they have someone on their side, or that the mediation process is more balanced. Some co-mediators have different backgrounds; for example, one may be an attorney and the other a therapist. These kinds of co-mediators then bring both sets of skills with them into the mediation, and the couple benefits from having two different types of professionals involved in the case. Co-mediation can be more expensive, though, since you are paying for two mediators' time.

Suggestions for Successful Co-Mediation

- Choose mediators who are experienced in co-mediation and have worked together before.
- Say something if you feel the mediators and your spouse are ganging up on you or making you feel outnumbered. This should not happen, and if it does, you need to point it out.
- Request separate rooms if you need to talk one-on-one with a mediator or if you feel as though you and your spouse are not working together well in person.
- Don't allow yourself to get lost in the discussion. Speak up and say what you want or what you think.
- Don't expect one of the mediators to be on your side. It's not a game of us against them. The mediators are supposed to remain completely neutral and are simply there to help you make agreements on your own.

Shuttle Mediation

Shuttle mediation is performed when the spouses have a hard time being productive while in the same room. If you and your spouse get upset when together, rile each other, or have difficulty focusing on the issues you need to resolve, but you want to avoid a courtroom battle, shuttle mediation might be a good alternative for you. Your mediator will schedule a mediation session; when you and your spouse arrive, the mediator may talk to you together in the same room to go over ground rules and procedures. Once the ground rules have been set and you and your spouse have both agreed to them, your mediator will place you in separate rooms. He or she will then talk to each of you separately and go back and forth in an attempt to reach an agreement. The mediator will look for points of compromise and carry settlement offers back and forth.

Sometimes shuttle mediation is used from the very beginning of the mediation process. Other times it is suggested by the couple or their mediator partway through when it becomes obvious that regular mediation is not working.

Shuttle mediation is often effective when regular mediation is not because it removes the conflicts you and your spouse have when you are communicating directly with each other. Instead of focusing on what you don't like about each other or what is making you crazy, you focus on the issues and how you can find mutually agreeable solutions. It is much less confrontational and gives you time to process what the other person is saying or offering before responding.

Suggestions for Successful Shuttle Mediation
- Be up front with your mediator about your ability to work in the same room.
- Choose a mediator you both trust.
- Have very clear ground rules about what the mediator can share from the private sessions with the other person. Sometimes being able to vent with the mediator can be very helpful, but if those words are shared with the other spouse, it may impede progress.
- Bring something to do while the mediator is with your spouse. Sitting and stewing about the mediation process can make you crazy.
- Don't expect the mediator to instinctively know what you want. Be sure to spell everything out.
- Stand up for what you want. The mediator will come back to you with suggestions or comments from your spouse. Do not feel intimidated into agreeing with them unless they are what you really want.

Attorney-Attended Mediation

Some mediators allow you to bring your attorneys with you to mediation. This happens only if both spouses agree. The attorneys listen to the negotiations and may take some private time with their clients to offer advice or information. This type of mediation works well when there are complicated legal issues involved and it would be too difficult to try to see your own attorney privately and explain the issues and options being considered. It can be time consuming, since there are more people involved, and it is more expensive, since you must pay the attorneys for their time. Additionally, some couples feel intimidated in the presence of attorneys and don't freely negotiate in this situation.

Suggestions for Successful Attorney-Attended Mediation
- Use this option only when necessary, since it will be quite expensive.
- Get permission from your spouse and mediator before bringing an attorney along.
- Be clear with your attorney about why you want him or her there and what he or she can do to assist you.

Long-Distance Mediation

If you and your spouse live far apart but still want to mediate, you might consider videoconferencing mediation. It is also feasible to use e-mail, instant messaging, or conference calls. The biggest problem is that the mediator will most likely be in the same room with one of you, possibly making the other spouse feel he or she is at a disadvantage. It can be difficult, although not impossible, for a mediator to control the situation and interpret signals if one party is not physically present.

Suggestions for Successful Long-Distance Mediation
- Choose technology that everyone has access to and is comfortable with.
- Be aware that some things are difficult to convey unless you are in person.
- Be very clear that the mediator will not have extra discussions with the spouse who is sharing the room.

Community Mediation

Community organizations, like the Better Business Bureau, offer free dispute-resolution programs. The mediators handling these cases are volunteers and may be interns or mediators who are earning practice credits. If you cannot afford a private mediator, these programs can offer you the benefits of mediation without the cost.

Suggestions for Successful Community Mediation

- Ask if the program has successfully handled divorce or family law issues.
- Find out about the experience level of the mediators who work in the program.
- Ask if there is a limit on the number of sessions or the length of sessions.

▶ *Words That Work* Thinking About Mediation

Instead of Thinking . . .	Think . . .
The judge will make a decision in our case.	*We will make all the decisions in our case.*
I want X, Y, and Z in the divorce.	*We can both get what we need.*
I want custody.	*We can continue to parent together.*
I am not giving him/her a dime.	*We both need to be able to survive financially after the divorce.*
He/she is going to have to fight me on X.	*If we look hard enough, we can find a solution that will work for both of us.*
I won't give up until I get what I want.	*We won't give up on mediation until we find solutions for every issue.*
I am angry because my spouse does/did X.	*We are going to focus on the future, not on the past.*
You are such a *&%$#.	*We might not love each other anymore, but we can still be civil and work through these problems.*

Understanding Limitations

Mediation is not the ultimate life solution. It is a very useful tool, but it can't solve all of your problems. Although mediation has some similarities with therapy and counseling (it focuses on talking through your problems, examining your needs, and finding solutions that work for your life), it is not designed to be used exclusively in that way. Mediation is a goal-oriented process, and its purpose is to move you through the decisions you need to make to end your marriage. If you expect it to do more than that, you may end up disappointed.

Mediation cannot:

- Heal you or your heart
- Help you find your path after the divorce
- Convince your spouse to stay
- Give you back your old life
- Get rid of depression
- Find more money than there actually is
- Change you or your spouse
- Reduce your debts
- Help your children heal

The Mediation Mind-Set

If you're considering mediation, you need to understand the type of thinking you'll use in mediation. Mediation requires you to think cooperatively. It's easy in a divorce to suit up in your war clothes and head out for blood. When you use mediation, you will be encouraged to stop and think about what you're doing and how it is going to impact the other person. You created this marriage together, and mediation allows you to end it the way both of you choose.

Tips for Thinking About Mediation

- Consider the amount of control, creativity, flexibility, and freedom that mediation affords you.
- Weigh the costs of traditional divorce against mediation.
- Look at the time frame of a litigated divorce compared to a mediated divorce.
- Think about the fact that mediation takes into account the emotional divorce as well as the legal one.
- Understand that mediation is the best way to reach a solution about parenting because it encourages cooperation.

2

Giving It a Try

Saying Yes to Mediation

Kyra and Robert separated for a year, and after several attempts at reconciliation, they decided to get a divorce. In their marriage Kyra had always been the one who called the shots. She decided what they were going to do, how they were going to spend their money, and where they were going to live. Eventually Robert started to feel he had no real voice, and this was part of the reason they split up.

Kyra suggested mediation. Robert was afraid that once again his opinion would be disregarded or ignored, but he agreed to go for a consultation. He asked the mediator if he could speak to him privately about his concerns. All three agreed that this was acceptable, as long as what they discussed was later revealed to Kyra. Robert explained to the mediator how he felt like he had always been trampled on and didn't think that he could speak up for himself in mediation. The mediator listened to his concerns and asked a few questions. He suggested they discuss this with Kyra to set some ground rules that would allow Robert some guarantees that he would have input.

The mediator rephrased Robert's concerns to Kyra and suggested some possible rules that would allow Robert's voice to be heard. Everyone agreed, and they began mediation. Robert still had a difficult time standing up for himself, but the mediator was careful to stop Kyra at times and encourage Robert to speak. They successfully completed mediation, and Robert finally felt as if Kyra had actually heard him and considered his opinions. He left the marriage with renewed self-confidence.

Mediation is an alternative that works well for almost all divorces; however, each person must make an individual decision as to whether mediation is right for him or her. Not only must mediation be right for you, but it also must be right for your spouse, since it is a cooperative process.

When considering if mediation is right for your situation, it's important to think about its pros and cons.

Are You a Good Candidate for Mediation?

In order to successfully use mediation, you must be able to:

- Negotiate on your own behalf
- Remain calm most of the time
- Understand your legal rights and options
- Be willing to make some compromises that can benefit both you and your spouse
- Commit to the time necessary to go through mediation
- Be able to pay the mediator, either by yourself or by sharing the cost with your spouse
- Hire an attorney to represent your interests and educate you about your alternatives
- Make a good faith effort to reach a mediated settlement
- Provide complete financial disclosure
- Be willing to consider alternatives and options you may not have previously thought of

The Pros and Cons of Mediation

Pros

- You make your own decisions about the divorce agreement.
- You can take as much time as needed to reach agreements.
- Mediation is less expensive than litigation.
- Mediation is a personal, face-to-face process.
- Mediation is much healthier for children because their parents are not constantly fighting.
- Mediation teaches you conflict-resolution skills, enabling you to work out future problems together without having to go to court.
- Mediation requires you to treat each other with respect and decency throughout the process.
- Mediation is less stressful than a courtroom proceeding.
- The mediation process moves much more quickly than a court proceeding.

Cons

- You must deal directly with your spouse.
- You have to take responsibility for your own decisions.
- You must compromise.
- You must be able to stand up for what you want and negotiate on your own behalf.
- You must work hard to make decisions.
- You have to leave emotional issues behind and focus on decisions that must be made.
- There is often a point in every mediation where one or both parties decide the mediation isn't working, and you need to be resilient and move on to other issues.
- There are still many attorneys who do not understand or support mediation.

Although almost every divorce can be mediated, it is not appropriate for all people or in all situations. You should not consider mediation if:

- There is any history of domestic violence in your marriage or relationship
- There is any threat of violence in your relationship
- You are afraid of your spouse
- You are unable to stand up for what you want and to communicate your views
- You will not agree to a divorce or separation
- You truly believe your spouse is hiding assets or income and will not disclose them during mediation
- Child abuse is an issue in your divorce
- One of you has a severe mental illness, a mental or emotional disability, or an untreated addiction to drugs or alcohol

These are important considerations because mediation can only work if both parties are free to negotiate with each other without duress and with a measure of trust that they will not be deceived, harmed, or threatened.

If you are in a relationship that involves domestic violence or child abuse, the most important thing is to get yourself and/or your children to safety. If you are in immediate danger, call 911 or go directly to your local domestic violence shelter (check your local phone book or call the local police department to get contact information).

26

Are You Ready to Mediate?
Even though you meet the criteria for mediation, you still need to consider if you are ready to mediate. Some people are ready to mediate their divorce from the very beginning, while others realize later in the divorce process that mediation may work for them.

Mediation can be an option you consider after you become dissatisfied with the traditional divorce process.

To find out if you are ready to begin mediation now, indicate whether the following statements are true or false for your situation:

___ 1. I would like to achieve a resolution for my divorce as soon as possible.

___ 2. I think I can sit, talk, and work with my spouse in a reasonable way.

___ 3. I am ready to consider options and alternatives.

___ 4. I believe there can be more than one solution to every problem.

___ 5. It is important to me that my spouse and I each have time with our children.

___ 6. Although I might be angry, hurt, sad, or confused, I understand for the most part that seeking revenge isn't going to help me.

___ 7. I am not afraid of or intimidated by my spouse.

___ 8. I believe I am capable of compromise in this situation or at least want to try to compromise.

___ 9. I am ready to live apart and separate from my spouse.

___ 10. I am in the process of accepting that the marriage is ending or over.

If you answered true to five or more statements, you are probably ready to mediate. If you answered true to fewer than five statements, you may not be ready to mediate just yet, but that does not mean that in a few weeks or months you might not be ready. Spend some time thinking about what stands between you and the ability to mediate and what you can do to change that.

27

Assessing Your Negotiation Skills

Part of a mediator's job is to help you and your spouse negotiate. The mediator doesn't choose solutions, but he or she helps you find them on your own. This may mean drawing out a spouse who is not very talkative or who isn't offering solutions or compromises. It's possible to go into mediation with limited negotiation skills and still come out with a good and fair agreement. However, you will likely feel more comfortable and achieve your goals more quickly if you have some negotiation skills when you walk in the door.

To find out how prepared you are to negotiate, answer true or false to each of the following:

—— 1. I am willing to listen to several points of view before setting my mind on one path.

—— 2. When I don't agree with something, I am able to speak up.

—— 3. I am able to keep some things to myself and not share everything I am thinking.

—— 4. I am comfortable with the idea that in order to get what I want, I might have to concede on some other issues.

—— 5. I am able to explain my point of view and defend it in a reasonable way.

—— 6. I don't sit back and let other people do all the talking.

—— 7. I have legitimate reasons that explain what I want from the divorce.

—— 8. I can admit when I am wrong.

—— 9. Instead of always seeing red when something doesn't go my way, I am able to take a step back and consider the situation.

—— 10. I think I have a good idea what my spouse probably wants the most from the divorce agreement.

If you answered true to five or more statements, you have good negotiation skills. If you answered true to fewer than five statements, you may need to work on gaining or honing some skills. If you are not feeling confident in your ability to negotiate, be sure to communicate that to your mediator before the process begins.

Overcoming Your Fears About Mediation

When you are considering whether or not to mediate, you will probably confront some of these common fears. But for every fear there is a resolution, as shown here:

- **I'm afraid I won't get what I deserve in the financial settlement.** Because you have complete decision-making power, you are free to accept or reject any proposal. You also will be able to talk to your attorney and get advice about what a court would probably give you, which should help you gauge what is reasonable for you to ask for.
- **I'm worried that my spouse will not disclose all financial information and will hide things.** Your state most likely legally requires complete disclosure. Both of you will need to sign statements that you are fully disclosing all financial information.
- **I'm concerned that I will be bullied into agreeing to things.** You have complete free will in mediation. The mediator is there to make sure you think through all options before agreeing to anything. The mediator will not take either side.
- **I think we're just going to end up having huge fights.** Mediation is a safe zone where you are allowed to discuss all of your concerns, but you are not allowed to belittle, insult, threaten, shout at, or swear at the other person. Your mediator may also give you explicit instructions about what you can and can't say to each other outside of mediation.
- **I don't want to break down and cry in front of my spouse or the mediator.** People express emotions in mediation all the time. Mediators are trained to handle these situations and can give you time and space to regain your composure if needed. Mediation is normally less emotionally tolling than courtroom proceedings and is sensitive to the strong emotions involved in divorce.
- **I don't think I can stand up for myself.** Your mediator is there to help both of you voice opinions and consider solutions. But you're the only one who can stand up for yourself, and the mediator will urge you to do so.

• **It's going to be too hard to talk about all of this.** Divorce is difficult no matter how you do it, but mediation offers a softer and more bearable approach to dealing with the issues. Mediators are trained to help you work through the difficult emotions you will be experiencing and to give you time and space to talk about all the issues that you have.

Talking to Your Spouse About Mediation

Once you've decided that you would like to try mediation, you need to discuss it with your spouse, since both of you must agree to use mediation. There are two approaches you can consider.

The first is to discuss the general concept with your spouse now, without having any details about possible mediators. You can show this book to him or her and allow your spouse to look through it to become informed about mediation as you have. The benefit to this approach is that it gets your spouse in on the process at the ground level. If you choose this approach, explain and emphasize the benefits of mediation, as listed in this book (see Chapter 1), and how these benefits pertain to your situation. Then present a plan for how the two of you can locate a mediator and each learn more about the process (see Chapter 3). The benefit of this approach is that you both start together from square one. The drawback is that you have to work together to get the process moving, and if you don't communicate well, this can be difficult. If you choose this approach, do the following:

- Create a plan for how to proceed. Will one or both of you search for mediators? Who will call to make appointments for interviews?
- Set up a time line you will follow for getting the mediation ball rolling.
- Spend time separately thinking about the mediation process and whether you both feel comfortable with it.

The second approach is to do your homework first and then talk to your spouse. Find a mediator in your area, and call for preliminary information, including rates and availability. If you have an attorney, talk to him or her about using mediation and whether he or she will work with a mediator. Once you have information and options, approach your spouse with the information. The benefit to this approach is that you face your spouse armed with answers to his or her potential questions and you've done the legwork—all he or she has to do is agree. The drawback is that your spouse may feel strong-armed into mediation and may feel that he or she didn't really get to make any choices, which, of course, goes against the very logic behind successful mediation.

If you choose this second approach, do the following:

- Explain and emphasize the benefits of mediation (see Chapter 1).
- Provide some basic information (such as background, education, and rates) about the mediators you have contacted.
- Stress that you only spoke with the mediator about rates and schedules, not about actual issues in your divorce (it is important that your spouse knows you have not "tainted" or prejudiced the mediator against him or her). Encourage your spouse to call other potential mediators for some firsthand information.
- Give your spouse time and space to think about mediation.
- Encourage your spouse to obtain information on his or her own from lawyers and mediators, as well as this book.

Whichever approach you choose, it is helpful if both you and your spouse have the opportunity to speak with the mediator on the phone before your first meeting. This can help you both feel comfortable with the mediator and gather some preliminary information about the process. More information on meeting with your mediator is discussed in Chapter 3.

▶ *Words That Work* Overcoming Objections

When you talk to your spouse, you can't expect him or her to jump on the mediation bandwagon immediately, and you can't expect him or her to take your word for things. Your spouse is going to have questions and concerns. Here are some common questions and concerns, along with the answers or responses that you can provide:

• **Having two lawyers and a mediator is too expensive.** Mediation is actually much less expensive than a regular divorce because we will work out the issues ourselves and not pay our lawyers for their time to do it. We will meet with our lawyers only occasionally, and there won't be any court time or trial preparation fees. The mediator will charge less than a lawyer, and the process will be shorter.

• **If you've already talked to this mediator, then isn't he/she already on your side?** The mediator doesn't take any sides in mediation. Most mediators will not talk to either spouse about the issues without both spouses present. We only discussed rates and availability. The mediator doesn't know anything about our situation. You should feel free to call him/her yourself and see what you think.

• **Why can't we just let our lawyers handle this?** You may trust your lawyer, but he/she doesn't know all the details of our life and neither does mine. If we can make these decisions together, we're both going to come out ahead.

• **I don't want to go to therapy. The marriage is over. This sounds like therapy.** Mediation is not therapy. The point of mediation is to decide for ourselves all the issues in the divorce. We aren't there to find out how to stay together.

• **It sounds too complicated.** Mediation is less complicated than a litigated divorce. You and I will determine what is important to us individually, and the mediator will help us understand the choices and offer possible solutions to satisfy both our needs.

• **I don't have time to go through all of this.** Mediation will actually take up less time than traditional divorce. We will meet with the mediator for about six to ten sessions, on a schedule that works for us. If we were to use lawyers, we would have to meet with them extensively and go to all the court appearances, not to mention deal with the phone calls and trying to get them to call us back. Most mediators have flexible hours and can meet with us outside of business hours, if necessary.

- **I don't want to deal with this.** But we have to, and mediation is the best way for us to work through the issues we have to decide. In mediation we can talk to each other like civilized people and not expect our lawyers to work it all out or let a judge we don't know make these decisions about us.
- **I don't want to spend any more time with you than I have to.** We may not get along, but going through a litigated divorce is only going to make us enemies. If we use mediation, we can put it all on the table and get it all figured out ourselves and not let a judge and two lawyers have control of our lives.
- **I don't have a clue about what you're supposed to do in mediation, and I'm not even sure what happens in a regular divorce.** The mediator is there to help us through the entire process. He/she will explain all of the laws and tell us what we need to decide and what the choices are. And we will each have our own lawyers who can tell us what kind of outcome we would have if we ended up in court and advise us on what is reasonable.
- **What if mediation doesn't work?** Then we can go back to our lawyers and go through the courts, but at least we will have tried and we probably will end up resolving at least some of the issues so our lawyers don't have to decide everything for us. We can choose to leave mediation at any time.

How Mediation Will Affect You

If you and your spouse go ahead with mediation, you will probably find it uncomfortable at first. Anytime you and your spouse are together, things probably feel a bit weird. But as the process moves forward, you will find that you are becoming more comfortable and confident about mediation and about the things you want to get out of it.

• **Mediation can help clarify for you what it is you really want.** It can help you take a hard look at all the financial issues and clearly see what you need and how your life will be once the divorce is over.

• **Mediation will have a positive effect on your parenting abilities as well.** When you mediate, you will think of each other as coparents, not as parents on opposite sides. You will see that the time your children spend with each of you is something they need and deserve. You will learn how to parent together by focusing on your children's needs and come to understand that it's really not about each of you but about your children and what's best for them.

• **Mediation will give you and your spouse a new set of skills.** Should you disagree in the future, you will be able to call upon this experience and know how to approach the problem, how to talk through it, and how to reach a solution without having to go back to court.

• **Mediation will give you complete ownership of your divorce.** Every decision made throughout the mediation process will be made by you. You and your spouse will have the power to make all of your own choices. When your divorce is final, you won't be left with resentment or anger that you didn't get what you wanted. You won't feel that a judge made decisions for you that were wrong. You won't feel that your lawyer didn't really understand what you wanted or that he or she failed to communicate that to the court.

Tips for Knowing When You're Ready to Mediate

You know you're ready to mediate when:

- You realize that traditional divorce can be a painful, oppositional process.
- You want to move forward and make the changes that will end your marriage.
- You are ready to face your spouse and talk through decisions together.
- You accept that divorce is always difficult but realize that mediation is a civil and reasonable way to work through the process.
- You may not know what you want in the divorce, but you know you're ready to find out.

3

The Perfect Match

Choosing a Mediator

Chris and Deanna were ready to move ahead with their divorce. Deanna had been reading a lot of books about divorce, and one discussed mediation as an option. She mentioned it to Chris, and he thought they should give it a try and suggested Deanna find a mediator. First Deanna called the attorney who did their real estate closing. She suggested that Deanna call the bar association. Deanna did that and got a list of names. The book she read mentioned that there are state and local mediation associations, so she did an online search and found one for their area, with members listed.

Deanna took a look at where the mediators were located and made a list of the three closest to call. She called their offices and got some basic information about fees and qualifications and set up free consultations with two mediators for her and Chris. One mediator was a therapist and one was an attorney. Deanna made up a list of questions to take with her to the sessions and tried to be observant while in each mediator's office. She and Chris both asked questions at the sessions. After visiting both, Deanna and Chris agreed that they felt more comfortable with the second mediator, so they scheduled an appointment.

Deanna and Chris felt ready to begin mediation because they had done a thorough search and asked enough questions to give them a sense as to whether each mediator was someone they would be able to work well with.

A mediator sets the tone for your sessions and guides you through the divorce process, so it's important you feel comfortable with the mediator you and your spouse choose. In most areas there are many mediators to choose from, so you have a variety of options. Consider the mediator's other profession (many are attorneys or therapists), the number of cases he or she has handled, and the different types of mediation he or she offers.

Types of Mediators

Mediators come in all shapes and sizes, although most commonly their professional backgrounds are either as attorneys or therapists. And while you can't judge a mediator based on his or her profession of origin alone, it is important that you evaluate mediators based on their skills, personality, experience, and training.

Mediators with backgrounds as attorneys or therapists have their own advantages. An attorney-mediator will have a very good grasp of legal issues and understands how your case might be decided should you go to court, while a therapist-mediator will be more experienced in helping people work through their emotions and can manage a couple's hostility, anger, and hurt in order to get to a solution.

You may be able to find mediators who are accountants or financial planners, although they are rare. This type of mediator is useful if your issues are financially complicated or sensitive. Clergy also sometimes work as mediators. When considering a clergy-mediator, be sure that he or she will help mediate a divorce and not a reconciliation (if that is what you want). Retired judges will sometimes act as mediators. They have an excellent grasp of the law and the ability to see solutions, but because they are used to calling all the shots, they sometimes may not be as adept at guiding the parties toward their own decisions.

How to Find a Mediator

If you already have a divorce attorney, ask him or her for a referral to a mediator. If your attorney is a mediator, you will not be able to mediate with him or her since he or she has already been retained as your personal attorney and has a conflict of interest. If you don't have an attorney or if you don't like your attorney's recommendation, you can find a mediator in the following ways:

- Call your state or local bar association for a recommendation (see Appendix B for a link to a list of state and local bar associations). Some maintain lists of all mediators, while others only refer to attorney-mediators.
- Locate your local or state mediation association (see Appendix B) and obtain a referral.
- Contact the Association for Conflict Resolution (see Appendix B), the national professional organization for mediators, for a referral.
- Ask family and friends for the names of mediators they have used.
- Contact your local Better Business Bureau's Community Dispute Resolution Program (consult your local phone book because these programs are administered on a local level) and ask for mediators they work with.
- Call your courthouse and ask for a list of available court-appointed mediators.
- Look in your yellow pages under dispute resolution, divorce, divorce assistance, mediation, or divorce mediation.
- Look in online directories, such as Mediate.com (www.mediate.com) or DivorceNet (www.divorcenet.com).

Make sure to find out if mediators pay to be listed in the directory (because then their inclusion in the directory is an advertisement and not a recommendation) and if they must meet any minimum qualifications to be listed.

Choosing a Mediation Approach

As discussed in Chapter 1, there are several different varieties of mediation styles—including co-mediation, shuttle mediation, attorney-assisted mediation, and so on—you can choose from. By far the most common approach is traditional mediation, in which you and your spouse will meet with one mediator in one room. But there are other options available, and one of these might be more suited to your situation. If you are interested in any of these types of mediation methods, discuss them with your spouse and potential mediators.

Mediator Credentials

When you interview potential mediators or obtain information about them, you will want to know their profession of origin (as mentioned earlier, many are therapists or attorneys). There is no required licensing of mediators in any state in the United States at this time. It's important to note that many states certify mediators to work in court-ordered or court-recommended mediation programs, but this does not mean that a mediator without that certification is not qualified to do independent mediation.

The American Bar Association and the Association for Conflict Resolution have begun a national study to determine if a national certification program would be feasible and useful, but at the time this book was published, no decision had been reached.

Look for all of these qualifications in a mediator:

- The mediator handles (or has handled) divorce or divorcing couples in his or her practice as an attorney or a therapist.

Attorneys (if they are still practicing as attorneys in addition to being mediators) should be members of the state or local bar divorce or custody committees or the American Bar Association sections; therapists (if they are still practicing therapists in addition to being mediators) should be members of the American Association for Marriage and Family Therapy or a state family therapy association.

- The mediator has completed a minimum of forty hours of divorce mediation training given by professionals in the divorce mediation field, usually other attorneys or therapists. The training should be specific to divorce mediation and should include domestic violence training.
- The mediator is a member of his or her local or state mediation association and/or the Association for Conflict Resolution. This shows that the mediator complies with the organization's rules of conduct for mediators and stays abreast of changes in the law and in the field of mediation.
- The mediator has successfully completed at least twenty other divorce mediation cases.
- The mediator has access to another professional mediator for professional consultations. It is common for mediators to consult on cases without revealing their clients' identities to obtain another point of view or suggestions for helping the couple successfully complete mediation.

You may wish to ask your mediator for references, but realize that since mediation is a confidential process, many participants may not wish to have their names given out as references, so even well-qualified mediators may not be able to provide references.

41

Mediator Standards

The American Bar Association, the Association for Conflict Resolution, and the American Arbitration Association have created model standards of conduct for mediators, which you can read online at www.mediate.com/articles/spidrstds.cfm or http://acrnet .org/acrlibrary/more.php?id=39_0_1_0_M. All mediators should follow these standards, though they are not legally required to. Read over and familiarize yourself with these standards so that you can ask potential mediators if they comply with them.

▶ *Words That Work* **Questions to Ask Mediators**

When you have the name of a mediator you want to consider, go in for a free consultation. This will give you and your spouse an opportunity to interview the mediator and decide if he or she is someone you would feel comfortable working with. Ask the mediator these questions:

• **What are your fees?** Mediators normally charge between $75 and $200 an hour, depending on your geographic area and the mediator's experience.

• **Is there a retainer fee?** Most mediators request a retainer fee, which covers the first few sessions and work done out of session (such as phone calls and document preparation). Most mediators accept cash or checks.

• **Do you have a written contract?** A written contract or agreement is recommended since it will clearly list all fees and your responsibilities, as well as the mediator's.

• **What kind of document will we end up with at the end of mediation?** The type of document will depend on your state and also whether or not your mediator is an attorney. If you have an attorney-mediator, you may have a document that can be filed directly with your court, or if your mediator is not an attorney, you will have a document that lists all of your decisions and agreements, which must be copied into a court document by one of your attorneys.

• **How many mediation cases have you handled?** You want a mediator who is experienced and has handled at least twenty cases to completion.

- **What kind of mediation training do you have?** Look for a mediator who has completed a minimum of forty hours of mediation training, as well as domestic violence training.
- **What relevant organizations do you belong to?** Mediators should belong to a state or local mediation association or the Association for Conflict Resolution.
- **How long were you or have you been a therapist or an attorney?** If someone practiced law or therapy for only a few months and is a newer mediator, it might be an indication that he or she does not have enough background to handle mediation. On the other hand, someone who worked as an attorney or a therapist for only a brief time but has worked as a mediator for a significant period of time is probably well qualified.
- **Why do you think mediation is a good choice?** Through the mediator's response, you will learn about his or her perception of mediation and get to know his or her perspectives better.
- **How many sessions do you think our case would take?** Typical cases run six to ten sessions, but the number of sessions can vary greatly depending on the facts of the case and personalities of the couple.
- **How often do you schedule sessions?** Most mediators suggest you meet once a week, but they are flexible to meet your needs.
- **What's your cancellation policy?** Usually mediators will not charge you for cancellations unless they become excessive.
- **Can you tell us a little bit about how the mediation process will work?** Through the mediator's response, you will learn such things as how he or she sets up sessions, what the mediator's approach will be, what order the issues will be decided in, and whether or not you will be given homework (things to work on outside of sessions).
- **How long will it take to finish our case?** Typical cases are resolved within a few months, but it is completely dependent on how available you are for meetings and how available your attorneys are. Actually filing and finalizing your divorce in court can take longer, and this is dependent on your state's process.

• **What kind of role will you play?** Through the mediator's response, you will learn about the type of mediation he or she practices and get a glimpse of the way he or she will run the mediation.

• **Will you go along with any type of agreements we make?** Mediators are there to help with the process and not to make value judgments about your situation or the choices you make. However, all mediators should refuse to draft an agreement that is so unfair it would not be accepted by the court or is blatantly biased toward one of the parties.

• **Do you use outside professionals, such as accountants and financial planners, if necessary?** Some mediators will bring in outside professionals if a case warrants it. Cases that are extremely complicated are best suited to this kind of help.

• **Do you have experience involving children in mediation?** Some mediators will suggest you bring preteens or teens to a mediation session to allow them input in deciding where they will live and how they will spend time with their parents.

▶ *Words That Work* **Questions to Ask Yourself**

After you have met with a mediator, ask yourself the following questions:

• **Were the waiting room and office comfortable?** It's important that you feel comfortable in the office since you will be spending a lot of time there. The office should feel private, and you shouldn't be able to overhear other people (nor should they be able to overhear you). Some mediators use rooms that have comfortable chairs and a seating area in which the mediator can sit with the clients, instead of behind a big desk. Rooms that are calming and comfortable will help you relax.

• **Is the mediator someone I can be comfortable with, can work with, and can be honest with?** If you have any reservations about the mediator, it is best to get them out in the open. Ask questions to clarify your concerns. You're going to be working closely with your mediator, and if you don't feel that this is someone you can trust with your situation, you will not be able to work effectively with him or her. If this mediator is not someone you are comfortable with, you should find someone else.

• **Can my spouse and I afford to pay the fees involved?** Having to end mediation because you can no longer afford the fees can be a frustrating situation. Before you begin, be sure you and your spouse can afford the cost of mediation. See the next section for more information about paying for mediation.

• **Can I imagine discussing (or my spouse discussing) personal issues candidly in front of this mediator?** It is one thing to trust a person's competence, but it is another to be able to lay your personal life on the table before that person. Make sure the mediator is someone you and your spouse feel comfortable opening up in front of and who doesn't make you feel judged.

• **Did the mediator treat us equally?** If you felt there was any bias toward either you or your spouse, this may not be a mediator you want to work with.

• **How did the mediator control the conversation?** Did the mediator guide you in your preliminary conversation? This can be a sign that your mediator is good at directing discussions. However, many mediators prefer not to guide conversations and believe in giving clients total control.

Affording Mediation

Although mediation is less costly than traditional litigated divorce, it can still be an expensive proposition, especially when you are in a position in which your finances are going to be divided. There are ways to make mediation an affordable option. Consider these solutions:

- You and your spouse can share the cost (see the next section for more about cost sharing).
- The mediator may be able to offer you a payment plan.
- The mediator may be able to space out sessions so that you and your spouse can save enough between sessions to pay for them.
- Your attorneys may be able to offer you a payment plan. Since part of mediation is consulting with your attorneys and paying them to finalize the divorce, being able to space out their costs can help.
- You can do the mediation now and then do the actual divorce filing later, once you've saved enough to pay for that.
- There may be a volunteer mediation program available in your community. Ask your attorney, or check with your state mediation association, court, or the local Better Business Bureau's Community Dispute Resolution Program.
- Work out with your spouse as much of your settlement as you can before going to mediation and then only mediate those areas you disagree on.

Expense Sharing

When you go to your first mediation session, your mediator will ask who is paying. If one of you is more financially stable than the other, that spouse may be the logical person to provide payment. But this is not necessarily always the best solution. Some couples feel more comfortable if they each pay half so there is no feeling of obligation to the other spouse. It is also important to note that one spouse can pay both attorneys' fees as well if one of you cannot afford an attorney (ask your attorney what your state rules are about this). If one of you can't afford to pay mediation fees, you could work out an arrangement where you trade an item of personal property for having the fees paid (for example, "I can't pay the mediator, but you can have the piano if you pay for it").

Another option is to split the cost of mediation. You can:

- Each pay the mediator half
- Pay the mediator out of a joint account
- Prorate the percent you will each pay based on your income levels

Your Rights and Responsibilities

Your mediator may spell out your rights and responsibilities as part of your mediation contract. You have the right to:

- Consult an attorney
- Receive complete financial disclosure from your spouse
- Be treated civilly by your spouse while in mediation
- End the mediation any time you choose
- Refuse to agree to anything you are uncomfortable with
- Bring up any topic or issue that is of concern to you
- Equally present solutions and options and have them considered
- Receive receipts for payments to the mediator and a complete accounting for his or her time and expenses
- Have your attorney review any document before you sign it
- Ask that your children be part of the mediation process
- Receive a copy of the mediation agreement and any settlement or agreement documents you sign during mediation

As a participant in mediation, you have certain responsibilities as well. These include:

- Paying the mediator (however you work this out between yourselves)
- Completing the homework assignments given to you
- Producing all documents requested by the mediator

- Providing complete financial disclosure
- Treating your spouse and the mediator in a respectful manner
- Considering all solutions offered by your spouse or the mediator
- Retaining an attorney of your own
- Making a good faith effort to reach compromises and resolutions
- Attending all scheduled mediation sessions

Agreement to Mediate

A sample agreement to mediate is included in Appendix A. Your mediator's agreement may look slightly different but should cover all the same basic points, including:

- Mediator fee (retainer, hourly rate, refund process, cancellation policy)
- Mediator's promise of confidentiality
- Your and your spouse's responsibility to provide complete financial disclosure
- An agreement not to dissipate or waste marital assets during mediation (in other words, not to take or spend joint assets during mediation)
- A statement that you and your spouse are voluntarily choosing to mediate
- A clear description of the issues you are mediating (at the very least, it needs to say you are mediating a divorce)
- A promise of the mediator's impartiality
- An explanation of who will be responsible for paying outside experts (such as accountants or financial planners) who are brought into mediation (normally all fees will be your and your spouse's responsibility, and an expert will only be brought in if you consent)
- Your right and responsibility to obtain independent legal counsel

Be sure to read the agreement to mediate completely and make sure you understand everything in it before you sign it. Make sure you receive a copy of the agreement after it has been signed. Be wary of contracts that:

- Do not include the elements just listed
- Allow the mediator to disclose information discussed or provided during mediation without your permission or a court order
- Include large, nonrefundable fees (all fees you pay must be accounted for in terms of the mediator's time or activities relating to your case; if a mediator told you that you had to pay $5,000 up front and you couldn't get it back if you didn't use up all the time you would be paying for, that would be a red flag)
- Allow your mediator to file your divorce papers with the court (when you file the divorce, one person is suing the other; your mediator represents both of you, and filing the divorce papers would mean he or she is representing only the filing party—this is a conflict of interest)
- Require you to sign away your rights to go to court to get a divorce or your right to an attorney

Mediation Methods

Your mediator has certain skills and methods he or she may use in mediation. Becoming familiar with these will help you feel more comfortable with the process.

- **Rephrasing.** You may find that your mediator often takes what you or your spouse says and rephrases it or repeats it after prefacing it with something like, "So what I hear you saying is . . ." or "What you want Jim to know is . . ." The purpose is to help each of you feel as if you have been heard and to clarify your point of view or a suggestion for consideration. Your mediator may also encourage you to rephrase things by asking questions such as,

"Help me understand . . ." or "Tell me more about . . ." or "Can you explain what is important about this to you . . ."

- **Redirecting.** If you aren't being productive or if you've run up against a brick wall, your mediator may steer you toward another topic. Sometimes simply moving away from a difficult topic will give you the space you need so that when you come back to it, you will be able to see it with fresh eyes.

- **Caucusing.** Your mediator may decide to meet separately with you and with your spouse, or with your child, if you consent. Sometimes people are more likely to open up about what they want or what is bothering them when they are alone with the mediator. If caucusing is used, be sure that you have an agreement about whether things discussed in the caucuses will be private or shared with the other spouse. (Note that this is different from shuttle mediation, in which the parties stay in separate rooms the entire time. A caucus is a short one-on-one session that is held only when there is a need for it.)

- **Turn taking.** Your mediator will have you take turns expressing your opinions, thoughts, emotions, and suggestions. In normal conversation people often jump in and interrupt each other, but in mediation your mediator will encourage you to hear each other out completely before responding.

- **Information offering.** Your mediator will spend a lot of time talking with you about laws and legal requirements. Your mediator is an important source of information and interpretation and will be able to present you with some possible unbiased solutions to consider. Note this is not the same as giving you personal legal advice.

- **Organizing.** One of your mediator's jobs is to help you get a grip on your financial situation. Your mediator will help you put together a complete budget and financial picture. This requires your active cooperation. It is important to be patient and wait for the mediator to cover all the important aspects, which can take some time. Your mediator will also help you organize a parenting schedule and property distribution.

- **Outsourcing.** Your mediator may find it necessary to bring another professional into your mediation. Accountants, pension experts, business valuators, and child psychologists or counselors can help you understand complicated situations, facts, or processes. See Chapter 4 for more information about working with these professionals.

• **Background discussions.** Your mediator may wish to get into the background behind some of your problems or issues. If, for example, you and your spouse are disagreeing about the parenting plan and many of your problems go back to a certain incident where one parent did not provide proper care, it may be necessary for your mediator to explore that past history with you, to help you work through it or base your decisions upon it in a rational way.

• **Allowing healthy anger.** The mediation process is very emotional, and it is not the goal of your mediator to slap a lid on your feelings. Rather, he or she wants you to express your feelings in a useful way. It is fine to be angry, hurt, sad, or scared. But it is important in mediation that these emotions are expressed in a way that furthers the process. Instead of using your emotions to hurt each other, you should use them to explain things and make reasons clear. Your mediator should be adept in helping you do so.

• **Turning to the future.** Your mediator will encourage you to focus on the present and the future. You are in mediation to make decisions that affect you today and tomorrow, not to try to resolve past issues. Sometimes it is necessary to explain things that have happened in the past (see Background discussions bullet earlier in this section), but generally your focus will be directed forward. Your mediator may gently redirect you by saying things like, "I understand how you feel about what happened, but how would you like it to be arranged in the future?" or "Let's think about what you can do to avoid those problems in the future."

• **Questioning.** The mediator is not there to find answers for you but to help you find them yourselves. In order to do this effectively, the mediator will often ask you questions and/or turn some things you say into questions. If you say that you have to have the pool table, your mediator may ask why. If you take one position and your spouse takes another, the mediator may ask you what other possible solutions other people might find. This questioning is designed to get you to think about your reasons for things and to stay open to innovative solutions you might not have thought of.

Red Flags

If you encounter any of the following situations, you should consider seeking another mediator:

• **The mediator says he or she will handle the mediation and also the divorce court process.** A mediator should not handle the divorce court process, even if the mediator is an attorney. Doing so would mean the mediator represents both of you as an attorney, and attorneys should only represent one spouse in a divorce case. The mediator's role should be solely that of mediator.

• **The mediator does not recommend that you and your spouse retain separate attorneys.** It is very important that you and your spouse hire separate attorneys. These attorneys will be able to tell you potential outcomes in court, give you personal legal advice, act as sounding boards throughout the process, and review and possibly prepare the final documents that will be filed with the court. The choice to hire attorneys is yours, but a mediator should always recommend that you hire them. You cannot hire the same attorney to represent you both since that would be a conflict of interest.

• **The mediator develops a personal interest in one of you.** If your mediator regularly sees one of you socially or your mediator has or develops a personal relationship with one of you, this is a sign that he or she is not acting impartially.

• **The mediator talks to you or your spouse separately about issues in the case without establishing a clear policy about these separate conversations (which are called caucuses).** Caucusing can be an effective tool during the mediation process, but only if the mediator and the parties have a clear agreement about it. The parties must agree that either everything they talk about with the mediator in a caucus will be disclosed to the other person or nothing discussed in any caucuses can be disclosed to the other party.

• **The mediator takes sides, tries to push you into certain solutions, or is biased in some way.** The mediator should be completely impartial and never take a side during mediation. He or she must be very careful never to point out that one spouse is wrong, to suggest that one solution is better, or to say what he or she would do in your situation.

• **The mediator does not intervene when you argue extensively or does not provide you with direction.** The mediator must act as the captain of the ship, keeping you both on course and focused. There will definitely be times when tempers flare or you feel like you're stuck. It is the mediator's job to keep things moving forward and get you back on track.

Tips for Choosing a Mediator

You know you've found a good mediator when:

• He is warm and friendly.
• You don't feel rushed.
• She completely explains the process to you.
• He has time to answer your questions completely.
• She focuses most of her professional time on mediation.
• His office is comfortable.
• Her fees are reasonable and within your budget.
• He explains how he will guide you through the process and makes you feel as if it is doable.

◀ 4 ▶

Expert Advice

Other Professionals Involved in Mediation

Lisa and Justin knew when they began mediation that they had a lot of complicated issues to work through, but they were confident that with the right help, they would be able to reach the solution that would work best for them and their family. When they began mediation, they each hired an attorney and spent some time learning about their state's laws and how a judge would likely decide their case.

Justin was a mechanic and owned his own garage and had IRAs and 401(k)s in his name. Lisa was a teacher and had a state retirement plan. The couple also owned a vacation condo in addition to their main residence. They realized they needed someone to help them understand the values of these various items and to help them consider what kind of division might work best for them. Their mediator suggested they work with a real estate appraiser as well as a financial planner, who also was an accountant. Through the advice of these other professionals, Lisa and Justin were able to create a settlement that maximized their assets and was fair to both of them.

In addition to your mediator, there will be other professionals involved in the mediation process. Mediation involves attorneys (unless you choose not to hire them against the advice of your mediator) and often includes consultations with other professionals, such as financial advisors and planners, appraisers, law guardians, and therapists.

Attorneys

If you do not already have one, your mediator will recommend that both of you retain separate attorneys. These attorneys perform several important functions for you.

- **Provide legal opinions.** Your attorney will give you an opinion about your case. Not only will your attorney help explain the law to you, but he or she will help you understand what kind of result you would be likely to get if you went to court. You're not planning on going to court at this point, but you still need to know what you can expect because it provides you with information about your alternatives. If you can't negotiate an agreement in mediation, you need to know what outcome you would be likely to get in court. The attorney can also help you understand how some issues are commonly decided. For example, your attorney can explain how child support works and how retirement accounts are often divided.

- **Act as a sounding board.** Your attorney is available to you throughout the mediation process and is a good place to go when you are not making progress in mediation. All discussions with your attorney are confidential, and his or her experience handling divorces makes your attorney a knowledgeable source. The terms you or your spouse ask for in mediation might not be realistic, might be difficult to implement, or might be something a court would not agree to, so go over these decisions with your attorney. Your attorney can talk with you about the decisions you are considering and offer some suggestions, advice, and alternatives.

• **Offer mediation support.** Sometimes it can be helpful to bring your attorney with you to mediation, particularly if you feel you are having difficulty speaking up for yourself or getting your point across.

• **Review your agreement.** Your attorney will review the agreement you reach and make sure that it is comprehensive, is complete, and protects your rights. He or she will also be sure it meets your state's requirements and will be accepted by the court. The court must approve your agreement, and your attorney will alert you to any potential problems.

• **Finalize your divorce.** Your attorney and/or your spouse's attorney will be involved in completing the necessary paperwork to finalize your divorce in court.

Finding an Attorney

If you do not have an attorney, locate one before you begin mediation. Choosing a mediation attorney is different from choosing an attorney for a contested divorce, and your priority is to find an attorney who is mediation friendly, believes in the viability and effectiveness of mediation, and is enthusiastic about it. Some attor-

---

▶ *Words That Work* **Questions to Ask Attorneys You Interview**

• How long have you practiced law?
• How many divorces do you handle per year?
• How many mediation clients have you worked with?
• Do you practice mediation yourself?
• What are your fees?
• If we do not reach an agreement in mediation, will you handle my court case?
• If I need you to come to mediation with me, will you?
• Do you believe mediation is a good choice in my situation?

neys do not believe in mediation, feeling instead that the courts are the best way to handle divorces. Some even believe that mediation takes business away from them, so it is important to work with an attorney who feels positively about mediation and is enthusiastic about helping clients through the process.

To find a mediation-friendly attorney, contact your state or local bar association. If you have already chosen a mediator, he or she can provide you with a list of attorneys who are mediation friendly.

Once you've got some names, talk to the attorneys on the phone or in person. Ask about their feelings about mediation and if they believe it is a good alternative. Then schedule consultation appointments with the attorneys you are considering.

Using One Lawyer, or None

Some couples are uncomfortable at the thought of hiring two attorneys and a mediator and want to hire just one attorney. It is possible to hire just one attorney, but that attorney cannot give you personal legal advice. The most common scenario in which having

▶ **Words That Work** **Questions to Ask Your Attorney During Mediation**

- How would a judge decide this?
- Have you ever had a case with a situation like this? How was it resolved?
- I'm thinking of asking for the house and having my spouse make half the payments on the mortgage. Does that sound reasonable to you?
- I'm having trouble explaining how I want the retirement accounts divided. Can you help me find a way to explain it better?
- Is this child support plan one the court will accept?

one lawyer works is when the couple does not have consulting attorneys during the mediation process (that is, the couple works exclusively with a mediator) and then hires just one attorney to finalize the divorce. However, this situation precludes you from obtaining personal legal advice.

It is also possible to not use an attorney at all. Your mediator can explain your state's divorce laws to you. If you are using an attorney-mediator, he or she will be able to provide the divorce agreement in a format that can be filed directly with the court by you or your spouse. If you contact your county clerk's office or check your state's website, you can find information about handling the divorce paperwork yourself. Many states are now making the process more accessible and user friendly.

Therapists

Although mediation helps you work out the legal issues in divorce, it is not designed to help you completely resolve emotional issues. Before coming to mediation, some couples try therapy to save their marriage. Therapy can also be an important tool during mediation.

► *Words That Work* **Questions to Ask Therapists**

- What kind of education and certification do you have?
- Are you experienced working with people going through a divorce?
- How often are you available for appointments?
- What are your fees?
- Do you participate in my insurance plan?
- What kind of therapy do you do?
- How will you be able to help me?

Couples Therapy

Although you are divorcing, couples therapy can be very helpful. The focus is not on fixing things but on finding ways to come to terms with the divorce and developing new ways to work with each other and parent together. Get a referral from your mediator or family physician. Couples therapy can also help you uncover and cope with many underlying issues and misperceptions, making it easier to come to a reasonable divorce agreement.

Individual Therapy

Many people going through divorce find individual therapy can be very helpful. Your therapist can help you cope with the divorce, regain confidence, improve self-esteem, and look to the future. You can work through anger, sadness, fear, and frustration with your therapist and come to mediation better able to focus on the issues. Therapy gives you a place to grieve, express anger and sadness, and learn tools to help you cope with all of these feelings. Get a referral from your mediator or primary care physician.

Pediatric Therapy

If your child is having a difficult time coping with the divorce, consider taking him or her to a therapist that specializes in working with children. The therapist may wish to see parents separately or together at various points in the treatment. Making sure your child is able to cope with the divorce is important, and getting assistance for your family can be an essential step. Get a referral from your pediatrician or mediator.

Financial Advisors

Because divorce is primarily a financial rearrangement (except for parenting issues), your mediator may recommend that a financial advisor, financial planner, or a specialist such as a pension expert assist with your mediation. He or she can help you:

- Understand tax consequences
- Get the most tax breaks possible
- Understand capital gains
- Understand retirement accounts and social security and how they can be divided
- Find the best way to divide assets and retirement accounts in your situation
- Decide what makes sense to sell and what makes sense to keep
- Consider whether you should sell or keep your home
- Understand the value of and assist you in choosing an annuity plan for alimony (a financial account that is set up to automatically make alimony payments; see Chapter 7)
- Understand the value of the other spouse's business
- Discuss ways to refinance or manage debt
- Create a financial plan for the future
- Plan for your children's college expenses
- Consider the value of life insurance

Your mediator may recommend a financial advisor or may request that you locate one yourself. Look for planners who have the designation CFP (certified financial planner) or ChFP (chartered financial planner) and always ask if they have experience working with divorce clients. Be wary of planners who seem to be there to push or recommend only certain financial products.

Appraisers

If you have a home, business, vehicle, or collection that needs to be valued, you may need to hire an appraiser. An appraiser will examine the asset and provide a professional estimate of its value, including a reasonable sale price. This information can then help you when you are working on your property division.

When hiring an appraiser, make sure he or she is experienced in appraising this asset. Provide the appraiser with as much information as you can about the asset. For example, if your home is being appraised, explain that you put in a new furnace last year or that your kitchen cabinets are solid wood, not veneer. If a business is being valued, get details about what documents the appraiser is basing his or her valuation on. Your mediator may ask that the appraiser present his or her findings during a mediation session.

To find an appraiser, ask your mediator and attorney for referrals. Check Appendix B for information about finding appraisers and appraisal information.

Custody Evaluators

If you are unable to reach an agreement about a parenting plan, you may consider obtaining a custody evaluation performed by a child psychologist. The psychologist meets with you, your spouse, and your children and creates a report that recommends who the children should live with and how much time they should spend with each parent. Custody evaluations are most common in contested court divorces and can increase the rift between you. The report will almost always point the finger at one parent and point out the negatives of both parents. Reading this kind of report can be very painful, and it can be very damaging to your parenting relationship if it is ever presented in court. Most mediators will recommend against the use of a custody evaluator.

Law Guardians or Guardians ad Litem

If your case started out in court and then went to mediation, you may have a law guardian (which in some states is called a guardian ad litem) assigned to the case. These attorneys are assigned to represent the children's interests in custody disputes. If one has already been assigned to your case, this attorney will need to approve any agreement you make about parenting. If you wish, you can invite him or her to come to a mediation session to discuss possible plans. Understand that the law guardian or guardian ad litem is not bound by your agreement with your mediator and can use anything discussed or presented in mediation (for or against you) should the case return to court.

Tips for Working with Other Professionals

- Be clear as to whether you, you and your spouse, or the mediator is hiring the professional and who will pay him or her.
- Write down contact information so that you know how to reach the professional.
- Make sure you understand the professional's qualifications and experience.
- Have a firm understanding of what the professional is basing his or her recommendations on.
- Discuss the use of any outside professional with your attorney. Professionals other than therapists and attorneys are not covered by a confidentiality privilege.
- Consider expert advice you receive, and use it in conjunction with your personal feelings and preferences to make decisions that work best for you.

5

On the Starting Blocks

Beginning Mediation

Renee and Michael went to their first mediation session nervous. They expected that they would have to sit down and start making decisions about the big complicated issues confronting them, yet they felt unprepared to do so. When they got there, though, the mediator started out by talking about the rules they would use in mediation. Hearing the rules helped them think clearly about how the process was going to work.

Next the mediator wanted them to talk about their current situation: where they each were living, how they were managing financially, and how they were sharing time with their children. They were still in the same house, and Michael was going to move out at some point, yet they hadn't figured out how to do that. The mediator helped them create a plan that allowed him to move out the next month, arranged for them each to see the kids on a regular basis, and did some intermediate financial planning with them that kept them both afloat. By the time they left the session, Renee and Michael felt greatly relieved and ready to move ahead with confidence and clarity.

Once you've made the decision to mediate and you've chosen a mediator, you're ready to get started with mediation. At this point in the process, everything can feel overwhelming. There are many decisions ahead of you that might seem daunting; however, your mediator will take you through the decisions step-by-step at a manageable pace.

Setting Up a Schedule

The first thing your mediator will do is set up a schedule. You'll schedule your first session, and possibly more sessions, in advance. Schedule your sessions for times when you don't feel rushed or pressured. Consider both of your commitments, responsibilities, and lifestyles when scheduling. If you know you'll be missing an important meeting at work or you'll need to hurry to pick up a child from day care afterward, you won't be able to devote your complete attention to mediation. Mondays can be a difficult day to mediate because they are often busy workdays. Some people feel too tired to manage sessions in the evenings.

Mind-Set

When you begin mediation, things will move more smoothly for you if you have the right outlook. Try to have the following attitudes during mediation:

- **Patience.** You might be ready to move forward and get this divorce over with; however, it is important that you do things carefully and in a cautious and reasoned manner. Rash decisions are often not the best. Your mediator has a reason for everything he or she does and says. You are paying your mediator to guide you through this process, so let him or her do this.
- **Flexibility.** Be ready to consider options and approaches you have not considered or to reconsider options that you have already rejected. Be willing to compromise.

- **Hopefulness.** When you are going through a divorce, it is easy to feel that you will never get past it, never recover, and never get your life back together again. You can and you will. If you are pessimistic, this attitude will drag the entire process down. Know that mediation is the path to a new life.
- **Open-mindedness.** Many divorcing spouses have set opinions about each other. In mediation you must move beyond these. Listen to what your spouse says, and give real consideration to his or her suggestions. If you can understand your spouse's point of view, it will help you formulate an alternative that might be acceptable to both of you.
- **Restraint.** Don't fly off the handle when you're upset. Instead, focus on communicating.

Ground Rules

When you begin your first session, your mediator will probably explain the basic ground rules that will be in place during the sessions. These often include:

- Do not swear.
- Do not shout or raise your voice.
- Do not interrupt.
- Be considerate of what the other person has to say.
- Arrive on time.
- Do not leave midsession.
- Let the mediator and other spouse know in advance if you must cancel or reschedule a session.
- Turn off cell phones or pagers while in the session.
- Complete all homework assignments.
- Discuss things in mediation before taking action.
- Agree not to file papers in the divorce or pursue the court case while mediation is ongoing. (Note that some mediators include this in their written mediation agreement.)

> ▶ *Words That Work* **Promises to Make to Yourself About Mediation**
>
> - I will not expect immediate results and will wait to see where the process takes me.
> - I will be ready to consider new options and avenues and will try not to become rigid.
> - I will assume that mediation can work for us.
> - I will give my spouse's suggestions real consideration and will not jump to conclusions.
> - I will remain calm and try to think things through whenever possible.

Immediate Decisions

When you begin, you may be ready to jump into discussions about pension plans and investment accounts, but there are other decisions that you will need to work on first. The first decisions you should focus on when you begin mediation (because other decisions will hinge upon them or they immediately affect your daily life) concern payment for mediation, living arrangements and expenses, and your children. It is not unusual to spend the first few sessions working out these issues. These preliminary arrangements can translate to something more permanent, so your work on these seemingly temporary issues can bring you closer to permanent agreements.

It can be helpful to have discussions about these issues before mediation. You may agree about many of these items, so you can come into mediation and tell the mediator what you have agreed on and then focus on the things you have not agreed on.

Payment for Mediation

The first decision you will need to discuss is how you will pay the mediator. He or she will help you work out an agreement about who will be responsible for payment. See Chapter 3 for a discussion of your options.

Living Arrangements and Expenses

You and your spouse must decide where you will both live during mediation and the divorce process. Some couples have already physically separated and don't need help with this. You also need to make temporary arrangements regarding joint household expenses. If you have not yet physically separated, decide on the following:

- Who is going to leave
- Whether one of you will remain in the marital home (or in the case of a rental, whether you will both move out)
- If one person is going to move out, where that person is going to live and how he or she will afford living expenses
- How you will pay joint household bills during mediation
- Whether there will be any income sharing during mediation

Your Children

If you and your spouse have children together, you must also decide on the following:

- How you will tell your children about the divorce, if you haven't already done so
- Where your children will live during the course of the mediation
- How you will share time with your children while mediation is ongoing
- Whether there will be any temporary child support during mediation

69

Some couples have no immediate plans to physically separate, because of financial concerns or for the sake of the children. This is perfectly acceptable, and your mediator can help you work out a plan that will enable you to live in the same house without driving each other crazy. Talk with your attorney before making a decision to move out, since in some states this can have serious legal consequences if you litigate your divorce.

Other Decisions

The first session can help lay ground rules for your interaction with each other outside of mediation. These agreements are not addressed in traditional divorce, but they are important, since they directly affect your daily quality of life.

Coping with Emotions

It is completely natural and expected to ride an emotional roller coaster as you work through important issues and face the future. Many of the topics you will be discussing and working through are filled with emotions. But in order to effectively move through the mediation process, you've got to get a business head on and carefully evaluate each decision. Divorce is a financial transaction. If you got emotional every time you went to the bank or bought groceries, you wouldn't get much done, and the things you did get done would probably not be done well.

▶ *Words That Work* **Sample Agreements to Make at the First Session**

- We will not take joint property without discussing it with the other person.
- We will try to avoid fights and instead work on resolving our conflicts in mediation.
- We will not destroy each other's mail or personal property.
- We will not harass or hang up on each other.
- We will not say derogatory things about each other to our children.
- We will not ask relatives or friends to intervene or choose sides.
- We will not enter each other's residences without permission.

You can't *not* have emotions, though, so learning to cope with them is an essential part of your divorce. No one ever succeeds in being emotionless in mediation. Expressing your feelings and being honest are an important part of the process, but the key is to not let your emotions control you. Deal with them outside of sessions, and use mediation to work through decisions, striking a balance between your emotions and logical decision making.

It is easy to attach emotional meaning to the inanimate items you will be dividing in mediation. But the china set is not your marriage, the gardening tools are not your self-esteem, and keeping the house is not the same as keeping a relationship with your children. Separate out the practical decisions from the emotional issues and stay focused when you're in mediation. Your mediator is there to help you do this, but if you can be aware of it yourself, you will move more smoothly through the process.

Developing a Good Relationship with Your Mediator

Many people enter into mediation with a feeling of distrust for the mediator and the whole situation, particularly if their divorce process began with lawyers and filing papers against each other. If you have a sense of uneasiness about anything related to the divorce, it will take a few sessions for you to feel completely at ease with your mediator. To help make yourself feel more comfortable, use these strategies:

- Always ask any questions that you have. Say, "Before we move on, I really need to know . . ."
- Ask the mediator to repeat something until you understand it, if necessary. Say, "I'm just not understanding how this will work. Can you maybe explain it in a different way?"
- Don't be afraid to comment if a situation is making you uncomfortable. Say, "I don't feel like this is something we

should be considering at all," or "I don't think that
bringing this up is going to help us at all."

- Make sure you understand the mediator's policy about
  caucusing (meeting with each of you separately). Say, "So if
  you and I talk in the other room, whatever I say will be
  revealed to my wife, right?"
- If there is something you are unsure about, ask for more
  time to decide. Say, "I think I just need to think about this
  a bit. Can we come back to it?"
- Tell the mediator about anything you are worrying about.
  Say, "I know we're talking about a parenting plan, but I am
  very concerned about how I am going to afford to live after
  the divorce, and I can't really think about anything else
  right now."
- Remind yourself that the mediator is impartial and is there
  to help you.
- Don't hesitate to talk to your attorney if there are things
  you need advice on. Say, "How is the amount of alimony
  usually decided?"

Improving Your Communication Skills

Mediation is all about communication. Remember that if you don't
say it, no one in the room is going to know what you're thinking
or what is important to you. There is no one else to speak up for
you but you. The mediator may try to draw you out or elicit your
opinion about things, but you can't sit back and wait for that to
happen. Follow these suggestions to maximize your communication in mediation:

- **Don't try to take charge of the mediation yourself.** The
mediator is the one in charge, and it is likely that if you try to lead,
your spouse may bristle. Instead of saying, "Let's talk about how
we're going to split up the investments," say, "I'm wondering when
we will get to the investments."

- **Use "I" statements instead of "you" statements.** Talk about what you want, what you think, and what you suggest, and stay away from drawing conclusions about what your spouse wants or needs. Instead of saying, "You always act like you know what the kids need," say, "It is important to me that I am involved in the kids' lives."

- **Focus on the present and the future.** Mediation isn't going to be able to change what has happened in the past in your marriage. That is something you will need to work on coping with yourself. What mediation can do is help you shape your future. Instead of saying, "You always were a tightwad," say, "I need to make sure that I have enough money to pay my rent."

- **Refrain from being inflexible.** Some people come to mediation with a plan already laid out in their minds about how the decisions should be made and then present it as if everyone should immediately agree. You're there to work out compromises. Of course, your spouse is not going to agree with every solution you present. Be willing to listen to alternatives and options before setting your mind on one course of action. Instead of saying, "This is the only thing I will agree to," say, "This is what I would really like to have happen."

- **Be brave.** It can be uncomfortable to consider paths or solutions that are completely foreign to you. Some people want to stick with comfortable, well-worn options. Just because you consider or talk about something does not mean it is going to happen. Being open to innovative choices or options you have not considered can help you find excellent solutions. Instead of saying, "That is so ridiculous," say, "I never considered that before. Let me think about it."

- **Talk!** Sitting there like a bump on a log isn't going to solve anything. OK, so you're feeling hurt, angry, betrayed, sad, or scared. That's normal. But try to talk about the issues at hand. No one expects you to come up with the grand solution. But nothing can be decided unless you take part in the process. Instead of saying nothing, say, "I would like to make sure I get the photo albums."

73

- **Talk to either the mediator or your spouse.** Some people feel as if they aren't supposed to talk to their spouse during mediation. It's perfectly fine for you to turn to each other and talk. And if you don't feel you can meet your spouse's gaze or talk directly to him or her, then it is perfectly fine for you to address most of your comments to the mediator (who may try to help you find a way to communicate directly).

Using Mediation to Solve Problems

Now that you have begun mediation, remember that it is there for you as a vehicle to solve problems. You and your spouse may encounter problems outside of sessions, and it is easy to fall back into old patterns of behavior to deal with them. However, now that you have mediation in place, use the communication, negotiation, and emotional skills you are developing. There may be some situations that need to be resolved on the spot, but there are also many others that can be put on hold until your next mediation session. Additionally, there may be some large issues that you are able to discuss and agree about on your own outside of mediation, but if you find yourself just butting heads when you try to talk about these things, it is best to wait until your next session to discuss them. If you continue to argue and fight about issues out of session, all you're doing is making it harder for your mediator to unravel them and defuse things.

Agreements

As you work your way through the mediation process, you will be creating agreements with your spouse. When you begin mediation, you may need to make some immediate decisions about where you will each be living, how you will pay bills, and when you will spend time with your children (see the "Living Arrangements and

Expenses" section earlier in this chapter). Your mediator may put this kind of temporary (nonbinding) agreement into a memorandum form and ask you both to sign it. If your relationship is extremely difficult and you have little trust for one another, your attorneys can take this agreement to a judge and ask the court to issue a temporary court order with the terms you have agreed upon.

The end result of mediation is a settlement agreement, which may be prepared by your mediator or attorneys. If the mediator will not be preparing a legal settlement document for the court, he or she will instead prepare a memorandum of agreement, which will be sent to the attorneys to be converted to a legally binding document.

Throughout mediation you may reach agreement on small issues that a court would not enforce, and these issues may not be included in your settlement agreement but will be agreed upon verbally. These verbal agreements are not going to be enforceable by a court but can help to clarify your relationship and iron out small difficulties.

Mediation Checklist

Your mediator may have a checklist for his or her personal use, similar to the one here, which lists most of the issues and topics couples generally need to discuss. Familiarize yourself with this sample checklist. Cross off items that do not apply in your situation. Add issues or decisions you will need to discuss. Place a check mark next to decisions you and your spouse reach on your own. Then share this list with your mediator and keep a copy for yourself. This checklist is a good way for you to keep track of progress in mediation and give you some notice of the things you have yet to cover.

You can also use the checklist to make notes briefly outlining agreements you and your spouse reach. This can be a handy reference and is especially useful when you read over your final agreement to ensure that nothing has been left out or changed.

Mediation Checklist
☐ Mediation Plan

Parenting Plan
☐ Decision making (sole, joint, divided)
☐ Living arrangements (primary residence)
☐ Time-sharing schedule ("regular schedule")
    ☐ Beginning and end, day and hour
    ☐ Notice of changes
    ☐ Travel arrangements and cost
☐ Holidays
☐ Long weekends
☐ School breaks (spring, Thanksgiving, Christmas, etc.)
☐ Summer vacation
☐ Birthdays (children's, parents')
☐ Other special occasions (Mother's Day, Father's Day, etc.)
☐ Other understandings
    ☐ Child care when child is ill
    ☐ Telephone access
    ☐ Gifts
    ☐ Travel (length of time, geographic location)
    ☐ Laundry
☐ Extended family
☐ Relocation
☐ Religion
☐ Decisions requiring mutual consultation
☐ Notification regarding illness, emergency authority
☐ Visiting if child is sick or homebound
☐ Access to school and medical records, sharing of address and telephone number information
☐ Provisions for review or modification
☐ Children's opinions

☐ Dating or sexual partners and impact on children
☐ Dispute-resolving mechanism—mediation for future problems

Support
☐ Child support
    ☐ Amount
    ☐ Time of payment
    ☐ Method of payment
    ☐ Emancipation definition
    ☐ Adjustments, increases, reductions, or suspensions
☐ Child care costs
☐ Summer camp, lessons, special expenses
☐ School tuition
☐ College
    ☐ What is child expected to do?
    ☐ What will parents do?
    ☐ What will be set aside now?
☐ Weddings, bar or bat mitzvahs, confirmations, graduations, other special events
☐ Spousal maintenance
    ☐ Amount
    ☐ Time of payment
    ☐ Duration
    ☐ Escalation, reduction, or suspension
☐ Medical insurance (medical, dental, optical, mental health)
    ☐ Who provides insurance for children and spouse
    ☐ Duration of insurance coverage
    ☐ Access to records, notification of medical problems
    ☐ Arrangements for submission to insurance and reimbursement
☐ Unreimbursed medical, dental, optical, orthodontic, and related expenses
☐ Life insurance
    ☐ Type
    ☐ Amount
    ☐ Duration

□ Beneficiary arrangements
□ Access to records, notification of changes
□ Disability insurance
□ Provisions for disability, unemployment, etc.
□ Need for financial planning for retirement, etc.

Property
□ Bank accounts
□ Notes receivable
□ Investments, stocks, bonds, mutual funds, tax shelters
□ Marital residence
    □ Duration of occupancy
    □ Mortgage or rent obligations
    □ Taxes, insurance payments
    □ Repairs
    □ Sale
        □ Price
        □ Listing
        □ Division of proceeds
        □ Buyout rights
        □ Fixing-up expenses
□ Other real estate
□ Retirement funds
    □ IRAs, TSAs, 401(k)s
    □ Keogh plans (self-employed)
    □ Pension plans
    □ Social security (if married ten or more years)
□ Business, partnership interest
□ Licenses and degrees
□ Other assets (tax refunds due, patents, royalties, etc.)
□ Personal property
    □ Cars
    □ Boats, RVs, etc.
    □ Jewelry, antiques, other items of large value
□ Household effects
    □ Division of items
    □ Provision for removal, storage

☐ Debts and loans
    ☐ Mortgage, home equity loans or lines
    ☐ Car loans
☐ Warranties (promises about there not being any other marital property or debt)

Other
☐ Income tax filings
    ☐ How to file (jointly, separately)
    ☐ Cooperation in filing, if joint; deductions, if separate
    ☐ Division of funds, assessments
    ☐ Prior year's joint returns refunds or assessments
    ☐ Dependency exemptions
☐ Future mediation fees
☐ Legal fees
☐ Estate rights waiver, need to revise wills
☐ Religious annulments and procedures
☐ How to proceed (immediate divorce or separation)

Organizing Your Documents

Your mediator will ask you to gather documents about your assets and debts so you can offer financial disclosure and provide a complete list of all assets and debts. Use an accordion folder or a plastic box with folders in it. Create separate categories, such as house, cars, health insurance, bank accounts, credit card bills, and so on. Your mediator will provide you with a list of the items you need to locate. You can also find this list in Chapter 8.

Tips for Getting Started Successfully with Mediation

- Go to the sessions prepared to move ahead.
- Remember that the only one who knows what will work for you is you.

- Keep in mind that your spouse is there to compromise.
- Bring along paper and a pen in case you want to make some notes.
- Write down questions that occur to you in between sessions, and bring them with you to the next session.
- Keep the mediator's phone number in a place where you can easily find it.
- Remember to bring the checkbook if you need to make a payment to the mediator.
- Don't expect to resolve everything all at once—have patience for the process to get moving.

6

Parental Guidance

Choosing a Parenting Plan

Rachel and Patel have a twelve-year-old daughter named Ina. Both Rachel and Patel wanted to spend as much time with Ina as possible, and they went to mediation without any basic agreement about how they would divide their time with her. The mediator had each of them clearly explain their work schedules. Rachel is a freelance illustrator who works from home, and Patel is a salesman who travels out of town several times a month. When they looked carefully at their availability, they agreed it made more sense for Ina to live primarily at Rachel's house, since Rachel was home most of the time. Both of them felt it was important for Ina to spend a lot of time with Patel, though. They talked about possible schedules but decided to bring Ina to a mediation session to get her perspective.

The mediator helped Ina talk about her activities and how important her friends were to her. Based on Ina's needs, Rachel and Patel created a schedule that enabled Ina to spend two weekends a month with Patel, as well as two evenings a week, which would fluctuate based on when he was in town. They agreed that Ina would continue all of her school and social activities, and whichever parent she was with would drive her to them. They also spent some time talking about how they would make decisions together as parents and continue to cooperate with each other.

After their divorce, they made adjustments to their schedule when necessary and talked every six months about how things were going and how they could better parent together. Ina spent time with both parents and felt loved and supported by both.

The less conflict that children are exposed to during a divorce, the better they adjust to the changes the divorce brings. Mediation facilitates better adjustment, communication, and mutual understanding of the needs of the children. Couples who mediate are better able to work together as parents after the divorce. While litigated divorces tend to highlight conflict between parents, mediation highlights agreement.

Mediation is an excellent way to determine where your child will live and how you will share time with him or her. Most mediators do not use the words *custody* and *visitation*, unless they are required in the court documents, because they feel that these words give the wrong meaning. Custody sounds like something that happens by force, and visitation sounds like something you would do with an acquaintance or friend. Instead, the preferred language in the mediation field includes words and terms such as *parenting time*, *parenting plans*, and *parenting schedules*. Language like this implies that each parent is an integral part of their child's life and future, no matter how much time each of them spends with the child. Gentle and fair language like this also helps defuse conflict, decreasing the frequency of finger-pointing and spitefulness. For instance, discussing possible scheduling options sounds much better to all parties, including the child, than discussing who will have custody.

Making decisions about how you're going to share time with your child is an emotional one, and your mediator will probably ask you to think about your lifestyles and schedules in deciding where your child will live and how he or she will share time.

What Is a Parenting Plan?

A parenting plan is a comprehensive plan that lays out how your child will share time with both parents and how you will continue to work together as parents. Your parenting plan describes everything that impacts your child, such as where he or she will primarily live, when each parent will spend time with the child, what rights the parents have in terms of decision-making power for the child's medical and educational needs, and the rules you will follow as you parent together.

When thinking about parenting plans, it is important to remember that it is about *sharing* time with your child, not about taking everything you can, winning, or making yourself feel validated. You created this child together and have probably raised him or her together. You're going to have to continue to parent together, and mediation can help you find a reasonable way to do that. It is also essential that you keep in mind that this schedule is set up to benefit your child. He or she needs time and a relationship with both of you.

Continuing Your Parenting Relationship

Although your marriage may be over, your parenting relationship is going to continue for the rest of your lives. It doesn't end when your child is a teenager, graduates from high school, turns twenty-one, or gets married. You will always be parents together (and you might someday be grandparents together!), and if you can learn now to make this relationship work smoothly, it will save you a lot of angst over the years. The goal is to create a blueprint for the way you and your spouse will parent together. Even if you decide you want to have very little contact with each other and want to parent as separately as possible, it is still essential that you create a plan for how you will manage pickups and drop-offs and how

> ▶ **Words That Work** Things to Say in Mediation to Help Develop an Ongoing Parenting Partnership

- It is important to me that you spend time with Cherie.
- I want to be able to talk to you about things that are happening in our son's life. I hope we can continue to make decisions together.
- I am committed to being parents even though we are no longer going to be married.
- I am not trying to cut you out of Christopher's life. It's important that he have a real relationship with you, and I am committed to making sure that happens.
- I don't think this is about who is a better parent. It is about what kind of arrangement we can make that will be best for Amanda.
- We both need to have a relationship with Kristen, and I really want to make sure that our feelings about each other do not impact her separate relationships with us.

you will interact when you see each other at school events and for other important milestones in your child's life. There is no end to your relationship as parents, and the sooner you can accept that and find a way to make it workable, the easier it is going to be for everyone involved, including your child. You are now and always will be a family. You aren't dissolving your bond with the other parent, but you are instead reformulating it. Establishing a parenting plan during mediation allows you to redefine your family for your child, so he or she will understand that although the family may be changing shape now, it is still a family.

Understanding Legal Terms
You may need to nail down some legal terms for use in your divorce agreement. The courts use a variety of words to describe parenting

situations. Because your agreement must be approved by the court, you will need to choose some legal wording to describe the arrangement you've agreed upon. Again, remember that these are not the ideal words to describe how you're going to be arranging things, but they do provide a clear definition of your plan. It is also important to understand that you might need two of these phrases to describe your parenting relationship—one to describe decision-making authority and another to describe how actual time is shared.

• **Joint custody.** There are two kinds of joint custody. *Joint legal custody* means that both parents have equal decision-making authority about the child. You can have joint legal custody when the child lives primarily with one parent or when the parents equally share time with the child. Most couples in mediation choose joint legal custody. This means that both parents will make decisions together about the child, and both have the ability to make medical and educational decisions.

> **Example:** David and Joan have joint legal custody of their twin boys. When one of the boys needed surgery, David was the one who took him to the hospital and gave consent to the surgery. When one of the boys got called down to the principal's office, Joan was the one the school was able to reach, and she went in and talked with the principal. Each parent has the power to make decisions about the children without getting consent from the other parent.

Joint physical custody is also called shared custody and means the child will equally split his or her time between the parents.

> **Example:** Shawna and Red each spend two weeks per month with their daughter, LaToya. If they also had joint decision-making authority, it would be called joint legal and physical custody.

• **Sole custody.** There are two types of sole custody. *Sole legal custody* means that only one parent can make important legal, medical, or educational decisions concerning the child.

Example: Lauren has sole legal custody of her son, Max. She is the only one who can decide where he will go to school or if he will get a fluoride treatment at the dentist's.

Sole physical custody means that the child lives with one parent and does not usually see the other parent.

Example: Todd has sole physical custody of his daughter, Shawna. Her mother lives in Asia, and she rarely sees her or has any contact with her.

• **Residential or primary custody.** This refers to the parent the child lives with most of the time. The child has visitation with the other parent.

Example: Marti has residential custody of her son, Nicholas. He lives with her most of the time and sees his father on weekends.

• **Visitation.** This is the time schedule for the parent with whom the child does not primarily live.

Example: Alex shares joint legal custody of his daughter, Emma, with his ex. Emma lives with her mom most of the time and has visitation with Alex on a regular basis.

How to Make Parenting Plan Decisions

Too often decisions about parenting plans are based on what the parents want. Although your schedules obviously are important, decisions about parenting time should be made based on what is best for the children. Courts rely on the "best interests rule." This means that the decision is made by determining what is best for that particular child in that particular situation. The decision is not made based on which parent is in the right in the divorce (some people believe that if a person is the one who brought about the end of the marriage, he or she should not be given custody). Mothers have no greater right to time with their children than fathers do. Your attorney or mediator can explain the standards used by courts in your state for making custody decisions so that you understand how judges make their custody rulings.

Parenting decisions are not about punishing each other, making a point, or winning. Instead, they should be about creating a plan that will give your child the best of both of you in a reasonable, manageable way. What works in one family's situation may not work in another. Mediation is the best way to make parenting plans because it allows you to custom design a plan to fit your family's particular style and needs. Conversely, in court, the judge will hear testimony and then, more often than not, offer a plan not that much different from the three others he or she has decided that day. You are the people who know your child best, and you are best equipped to make a decision about how your child should share time with you.

Factors to Consider in Deciding Parenting Plans

When working with your mediator to create your parenting plan, you must first think about where your child will primarily live. Consider:

- Your schedule and availability
- Your spouse's schedule and availability
- Where you each will be living and how far apart your residences are
- What school your child goes to now and which school district you will each be living in after the divorce
- What type of home you will each be living in and how large each house is

Your mediator will discuss these factors with you, and as you talk them through, it is likely that a basic plan is going to emerge. For many families, though, the answer to this basic layout is not a simple one. You and your spouse may both feel as though you want your child to live primarily at your respective homes. If you absolutely can't seem to come to an agreement, you might want to consider shared parenting, where you share your time equally with your child.

In most cases, the least amount of disruption in your child's life, the better off he or she will be. If your child can continue to live in the same home and go to the same school, it will make adjustment much easier. This isn't always possible or desirable, though, so you have to do what works best in your situation. It is important to remember that the decision about where your child will live is not a commentary on who is the better parent. It is instead a decision that has to do with what works best for your child. Both of you will continue to be parents and be involved in your child's life. You're not making a decision that leaves your child with one parent. Instead, you are trying to maximize each parent's availability so your child is able to spend quality time with both of you.

Creating a Schedule

When you create a schedule, you will be deciding the details of where your child will be when. Most people believe it is important for a child to have frequent contact with both parents each week, but you can create any schedule that works for your family. Weekends and evenings are often the key times, since that is when both parents and children usually have free time. But don't forget about after school and before school—these may be short time periods, but they are important times for your child. Both of you are going to continue to live with your child, and this means sharing the fun times as well as the everyday times. One parent shouldn't be the boring "clean your room and do your homework" parent while the other parent is the "let's go to the amusement park this weekend" parent. Both of you should be involved in all facets of your child's life.

To begin to think about what kind of schedule will work, consider your and your spouse's work schedules. If one of you works from 9 A.M. to 5 P.M. and the other from 6 P.M. to 2 A.M., it makes sense for your child to have scheduled time with each of you when you are not working. Otherwise, your child is just going to be with a sitter during that time. Consider how far apart you will be living and how easy it will be to transport your child from one home to the other. Consider your child's personality. Some children have no problem with change and are happy to move between parents' homes several times a week. Other children function better with fewer changes.

You, your spouse, and your mediator will begin to map out a tentative schedule. It may take a few sessions to work this out completely. When working out your regular parenting schedule, consider:

- When you each have free time you could spend with your child
- How regular your work hours are (and if overtime or unexpected additional hours are common) and what kind of commuting time is involved
- How you can arrange things so your child has adult supervision after school, at night, and on weekends
- Ways to maximize your child's time with each of you
- Methods for minimizing day care and baby-sitting costs (by arranging things so your child is with an available parent when possible instead of with a sitter)
- Scheduled activities that are important and meaningful for your child to continue
- Where your child goes to school and what his or her homework load is like (if there is a lot of homework, this means either scheduling times with the nonresidential parent on weekends or understanding that your child will be doing homework during scheduled parenting time— something that actually gives things a sense of normalcy)

Discuss phone and e-mail contact with the other parent. If your child knows he or she is free to pick up the phone and talk to the other parent, it can help make the adjustment process smoother.

How to Make a Schedule

When thinking about a schedule, you need to use several calendars. You and your spouse should have your individual calendars out. If you have a school calendar or calendar with your child's activities on it, that will also be important. Your mediator will most likely have a master calendar on an easel or on the table in front of you so that you can see the parenting schedule you are creating or discussing. Using these visual aides will help you think clearly about the plan.

If you're having trouble thinking in large-scale terms (and it can be pretty overwhelming to try to figure out how you're going to plan a schedule for the next year, let alone the next ten years), try instead to think about the next week and the week after that. If you take things one week at a time when you first begin discussing a schedule, a pattern will probably begin to emerge, and you can then apply it to the rest of the year.

Holiday Schedules

In addition to your schedule of daily life, you will need to create a holiday and vacation schedule. You have complete freedom when creating this schedule. The first thing you will need to do is create a list of holidays you want to share with your child. You may want to include some of the following:

- New Year's Day
- Easter
- Passover
- Memorial Day
- Mother's Day
- Father's Day
- Your child's birthday
- Your birthday

- The other parent's birthday
- Fourth of July
- Labor Day
- Rosh Hashanah
- Yom Kippur
- Halloween
- Thanksgiving
- Hanukkah
- Christmas Eve
- Christmas Day
- Kwanzaa
- Ramadan
- Other holidays you celebrate or want to share with your child

Some parents choose to alternate holidays (this year you get New Year's Day and your ex gets Valentine's Day, since it is the next holiday in your rotation), while others choose to create a set schedule that will be the same every year (you get Thanksgiving and the other parent gets Christmas Day every year, for example). When you are working out a holiday schedule, think creatively. You can split a day into two parts, celebrate something the day after the traditional holiday (after all, a holiday is really when you make it), and even spend some holidays all together as a family. (Particularly in the first few years after the divorce, some parents choose to spend Christmas morning together.) What works for you this year might not be what will work next year, so be sure to keep an open mind.

In addition to holidays, plan out how you will share your child's vacation time. One of you may want to take a trip with your child during winter or spring break. Some parents like to split up the summer in weekly blocks, while others like to have their child for an extended period over the summer with no interruptions.

Key Points to Remember When Creating Schedules
While you will be creating a schedule that is tailored to your situation, there are some important basics to keep in mind:

- **Children need routines.** Create a plan that does not fluctuate or bounce around too much. Kids need to know where they're going to be when. A schedule that has a child at Mom's on Monday and Friday this week, Tuesday and Wednesday next week, and Thursday and Saturday the week after is going to be too confusing for most children.

- **Many children need a home base.** While both of your homes are going to be "home" to your child, many children really need one home at which they spend a majority of their time. Some kids are able to thrive in a true shared custody arrangement, but many kids simply feel too unstable basically living out of a suitcase.

- **Different ages have different needs.** For example, babies and toddlers live by routines and need frequent contact with both parents. Teenagers live by their social schedule, and it is essential to make sure they have time for their activities, friends, and jobs.

- **Needs change.** As your child grows, he or she is going to have different needs and a different schedule. Your job as parents is to try to accommodate that as best you can by making adjustments in your parenting schedule.

- **Parents are not perfect.** You're both going to goof up sometimes, and if you can agree to support each other in your parenting no matter what, things will go much more smoothly.

- **Be flexible.** The best-laid plans can fail or need adjustment. No matter how well you plan out a schedule, there are going to be times when it just doesn't work. Things come up, plans change, and people need forgiveness. Be flexible and be forgiving. Build a schedule, but make plans for how you will ask each other for changes and how you will make adjustments when needed.

92

Involving Your Child

Mediation offers you the opportunity to involve your older child in the parenting plan discussions. Children age ten or older may be mature enough to attend a mediation session and voice their opinions and desires. Consider including your child in a mediation session if:

- Your child is not afraid or nervous at the idea of it
- You and your spouse believe you can treat each other civilly
- Neither one of you will pressure your child about what he or she will say
- You and your spouse are able to help your child understand that he or she is not going to be put on the hot seat, punished, asked to make a choice, or made to feel bad while in mediation or afterward
- Your child is mature enough to understand what mediation is about and how he or she can participate
- You and your spouse can recognize when your child's presence or opinion is no longer useful or productive
- You and your spouse are able to handle hearing your child's honest opinion and preference

It can be helpful to get your child's input if you are having trouble deciding on a primary residence or if you're having some difficulty creating a schedule to follow. But you, your spouse, and your mediator should never put the burden on your child to make a choice or let your child think the responsibility is his or hers to make the decision about the parenting plan. Only the parents can make the decision, although the child can offer input. The mediator may wish to speak to the child separately, but only if both parents agree. This can help a child talk more freely. Sometimes when confronted by both parents, children are afraid to say what they really think because they don't want to hurt either parent.

If you will be bringing your child along to a mediation session in which you will discuss your parenting plan, do these things to help make the session productive:

- **Prepare your child in advance.** Explain to him or her who the mediator is and what the mediator is helping you do. Talk about what you will be doing at the mediator's office and why your child is invited. Stress that your child is there to share his or her feelings and that he or she is not going to be on the spot.
- **Be prepared to listen.** You are not there to argue, blame anyone, or get into any other issues during the session.

- **Have reasonable expectations.** Don't expect to reach a solution at this session. View it instead as a fact-finding mission and a chance to float some alternatives.
- **Be conscious of what you say.** Try to avoid using the words *custody* and *visitation* in this session. You may need to make a decision about these words if it is required in your state, but save that for another time. Children don't need to think of themselves as possessions that are owned or negotiated over.
- **Keep mum about money.** Don't discuss child support or other financial matters during this session.

Other Decisions

Once you've created a schedule, you may need to make some other related decisions. These can include:

- What items will travel back and forth with your child (such as backpacks, favorite blankies or stuffed animals, toys, pacifiers, cell phones, etc.)
- When and how you will work out changes to the schedule (by phone, in person, by e-mail, etc.), as well as how much notice you want to try to give each other for requests of changes
- Whether you will have a yearly review to determine if the schedule you have in place will continue to work
- Who will attend school performances, sports events, and teacher conferences
- Whether you want to consult each other about buying birthday and holiday gifts for your child (some parents purchase large items together or at least compare lists to make sure they aren't buying duplicate items)
- Who is responsible for answering notes, permission slips, and other communication from school and coaches, as well as invitations to birthday parties (some parents have the residential parent handle these things, while other parents make each parent responsible for things that will happen during his or her scheduled time)

- What will happen when your child is home sick or school is closed due to inclement weather
- Using each other as the first baby-sitter of choice before calling someone else
- Making time in the child's life for grandparents and extended family
- Who will schedule and take the child to haircuts, dental appointments, and well visits
- How you will handle last-minute and emergency scheduling problems (for example, if one parent is stuck in a bad traffic jam or is held up at work)

Keeping Parenting Separate

While it is true that all of the decisions you will make in mediation are intertwined in some way, you really need to make an effort to keep your parenting plan separate from other decisions, because it is not fair to use your child as a pawn to get a better property settlement or to insist on having custody just so you can get child support payments. The following things should not be a factor in your parenting plan discussions:

- Child support
- Property settlements
- Fault for the divorce
- Alimony
- Debts
- The legal reason for the divorce

Focusing on Details

It is often the details and small points that become the biggest problems with living with a parenting plan. Once you've hammered out a satisfactory schedule, there are some other things you need to think about, which your mediator can help you work on. Here are some small points you should think about and discuss in mediation:

- **Transportation.** Who drives which way? Will the person with the child be the one responsible for taking the child to the other parent, or will the parent who is waiting for the child come and get the child?

- **Tardiness.** How big of a window will you allow for lateness? Will you expect a phone call if the other person will be more than fifteen minutes late?

- **Entering homes.** Will you come into each other's home or exchange your child on the doorstep, in the driveway, or on the sidewalk?

- **Laundry.** Who will wash the clothing the child wears when at the different homes? Will it be returned at the end of that visit or the next visit? Believe it or not, children's laundry is one of the most common problems divorced parents argue about.

- **Forgotten items.** If your child leaves an essential item (anything from a pacifier to homework to a cell phone, depending on the age) at the other home, how will you get it back to the child?

- **Phone calls.** Most parents agree that their child can have phone contact with both parents, but how much is too much? If your ex calls every hour during your time, is that excessive?

- **Schedule changes.** If one of you needs to make changes to the schedule, how much notice do you need to give each other? How often can you make changes?

- **Activities.** Will parenting time interfere with your child's activities? If a child wants to plan an activity during one parent's time, does the child need to get permission from that parent? Do you need to consult before signing a child up for a long-term activity that will impact both of your times?

- **Meals.** If a pickup/drop-off is scheduled near a mealtime, clarify where the child will be eating so you can avoid one parent preparing a meal and being disappointed to find the child has already eaten. With younger children, will you communicate with each other about how much the child has eaten or drunk while with you?

- **Illness.** When is a child too sick to go with the other parent? If your child is seriously ill, will you arrange for the other parent to come and spend some time with him or her?

- **Visits with friends.** Will your child be able to have friends over and go to friends' houses while at each of your homes?
- **Discipline.** Will you have the same rules in each home or each formulate your own rules? If a child is grounded at one home, will the grounding be in effect at the other home? In general, it is best if you can closely coordinate household rules and stand together as a united front.

Frozen Embryos

If you and your spouse have frozen embryos that you created during fertility procedures, you can use mediation to discuss what will happen to these, such as:

- Whether one spouse will be given ownership and the ability to implant them
- What your responsibilities will be to each other if these embryos are used by one of you (for example, will the other parent have to pay child support, and will he or she be allowed to spend time with the child?)
- Whether you want to destroy them or donate them to research or to infertile couples

Tips for Creating Workable Parenting Plans

- Remember that, first and foremost, a parenting plan is supposed to give your child a settled, dependable way to have a real relationship with both parents.
- Before you can create a plan that works, you must accept the fact that you will be sharing your child with the other parent.
- The best way to create a long-term plan that will work is to realize that nothing you decide today can be completely permanent. Your plan must change as your lives and your child's life change.

- Tell yourself that spending plenty of time with each parent is something that is essential to your child's development.
- Resolve to create a partnership with the other parent, to work together for your child's benefit.
- Time is what you make of it. Taking your child out to breakfast once a week might not seem like something important, but if you do it every week, it becomes important.
- If you don't see your child every day or every week, make sure that when you do spend time together, you do things that are normal—like washing the dishes or watching TV together. You shouldn't focus on being an entertainer or trying to be the favorite parent, but instead you should focus on creating a real life with your child.

7

Money Talks

Mediating Child Support and Alimony

Chantal and Mark have three children, each with very different needs and expenses. Their youngest, Tyler, is still wearing diapers and goes to day care. Their middle child, Maddy, is in elementary school and takes dance lessons and goes to Girl Scouts. Their oldest, Katrina, is in high school and is looking at colleges, is learning to drive, is searching for a job, and is a cheerleader. Before the divorce, Chantal was a stay-at-home mom who sometimes did clerical work at Mark's medical practice.

Chantal and Mark have decided to share joint custody, with all three children primarily living with Mark in the home the family lived in before the divorce. Chantal is moving in with her mother in another town and will go back to school. Because of their out-of-the-ordinary situation, Chantal and Mark felt that traditional arrangements weren't going to work for them. In mediation they were able to be creative about child support and alimony.

Chantal is going to see the kids every other weekend and for extended periods during her semester breaks, when she will move back into the apartment above the garage. Because Mark is highly paid and Chantal is going to be a student, he told her during their mediation session that he did not want to accept any child support. Chantal, however, felt very strongly about participating financially in her children's lives. They agreed she would pay $20 a week while she is in school and then renegotiate once she has a career. This made her feel like she was contributing to her children's lifestyle. They agreed that Mark would pay for the children's health and education expenses; however, Chantal will take them shopping and put the bills on a credit card that Mark will pay.

Mark is going to pay Chantal's tuition bills as part of their settlement, and she will not receive any alimony. She will be able to use the apartment over the garage whenever she wants to so that she can be near the children. Mark will pay half the utilities for that apartment, and Chantal will be responsible for furnishing and decorating it. Chantal will also continue to come into Mark's office once a week and do filing.

Alimony and child support can be contentious, even when everything else in mediation has gone fairly smoothly. When discussing property settlements, both parties usually feel they are getting things they want, but with alimony or child support, a feeling of unfairness can dominate, and it can seem as if one person is winning while the other is paying. When arranging for payments on a long-term basis, tempers tend to flare. You're in mediation because you want to end your obligations to each other, not continue them. However, child support and alimony are sometimes necessary to make sure the other spouse and children of the marriage can survive. Mediation can help you make decisions about payments in a way that considers everyone's needs.

Alimony

Alimony is a payment made from one spouse to the other. In most situations, alimony is about support, not about punishing or penalizing one of the spouses. Courts usually order alimony when:

- One spouse needs support while he or she gets an education, looks for a job, reenters the workforce, or makes a career change
- One spouse is permanently disabled in some way
- One spouse is elderly
- There is a very significant difference between the spouses' incomes

Your attorney or mediator can explain the standards used by courts in your state for determining alimony. In general, courts look at:

- The length of the marriage
- Each person's health
- Each person's income and earning ability and potential
- The property each is getting
- How they contributed to the marriage (for example, if one was an at-home parent or a spouse who stayed home and ran the home)
- Where the children live
- How the spouses have treated each other and the marital property (meaning whether or not one spouse hid assets or went out and spent a lot of money during the divorce)

Alimony can be paid to either spouse and can be for any length of time. Courts, however, usually limit alimony to one-third the length of the marriage, although lifelong alimony is not uncommon for older or disabled spouses. Alimony can be payable in any intervals you agree on: weekly, bimonthly, monthly, annually, and so on.

Because you have chosen to mediate, you have more freedom to custom-build your alimony settlement, which means that while considering the factors just mentioned, you can also base your decision on any circumstances that seem important to you and your situation.

The easiest way to begin alimony discussions or negotiations is to look at each of your budgets. If one spouse has a low income, few assets, and high bills and simply has no way to make ends meet, you may wish to think about alimony as a solution. If one spouse supported the other while he or she got a degree or began a company or practice and that spouse now has a high income, you may consider alimony as a way to compensate for that.

Alimony and Property

Consider alimony hand in hand with your property settlement. There are plenty of trade-offs and negotiations between the two. For example, you could decide to give one spouse a greater share of the investments, instead of creating an alimony agreement. Or you might decide to split assets in more of an equal way and set up alimony while one spouse works on reentering his or her career after years at home caring for the children.

Alimony and Taxes

Alimony is taxable income, meaning it is taxable by the person receiving it and tax deductible by the person paying it. When you're weighing property division against alimony, look at the tax consequences of options you are considering. Not only must you consider the fact that alimony is taxable income, but you also need to take into consideration the tax consequences of your property settlement (because some assets will have tax consequences; see Chapter 8 for more information). Your mediator may be able to walk you through some of these concerns, or he or she may recommend that an accountant evaluate your situation and come to a mediation session to discuss it with you.

Alimony as a Debt

Alimony cannot be discharged in bankruptcy. If one spouse owes alimony to the other and files for bankruptcy, alimony is not a debt that the bankruptcy court can wipe out, like a credit card debt. Some people do not realize this and enter into alimony agreements, thinking they will go bankrupt and get out of having to make the payments.

▶ *Words That Work* **Talking with Your Spouse About Alimony**

- I need alimony for a short time so that I can find a good job and be prepared to face the world as a financially independent person.
- I'm willing to pay alimony, but we have to talk about how we're going to divide up our assets before I can agree to any amount.
- I think that you don't want to pay alimony because you don't think I played any part in you getting your law degree. But I supported you through school, and I am asking you to support me for a short time so I can have a chance at a career, too.
- I want you to know that I'm not out to get you and I'm not trying to get revenge. But alimony is something I need to consider.
- I understand that we have to work something out so you can become financially stable. I just think there are options other than alimony that we should consider.

Factors to Consider

In most states alimony is not paid or received perpetually. You can create an agreement that terminates alimony in a variety of situations. Some you might want to consider are when:

- The person receiving alimony gets a degree or a job
- The person receiving alimony cohabitates with someone else
- The person receiving alimony earns more than a certain amount
- The person paying alimony retires

Alimony will automatically end when the person receiving it remarries or either party dies. Because of this, the length of

Tips for Mediating Alimony

- If you're the one who may be paying alimony, try not to look at it as a punishment. Consider it for the short term to assist your spouse in becoming more independent so that your future ties to him or her will be minimal. In the long run, think of this as a tax-deductible settlement.
- If you are seeking alimony, and really need it, don't give up. Present yourself as a reasonable person who will use the money to achieve something greater or better for yourself. Alimony is not something that should be taken advantage of, and often the spouse in the financially secure situation is cautious of being "taken to the cleaners," which is why he or she may refuse to give in without argument. If alimony is something you need to survive and your attorney believes you have a good argument, stand up for yourself and make your position clear. Laying out a clear plan for your future and how the money will help you get there will help create an agreeable settlement.
- Don't consider alimony in a vacuum. Always consider your property division, living arrangements, life plans, and other factors. You're trying to create a plan to help one spouse survive financially, and to do this you must consider everything that impacts both of your financial situations.
- Get an accountant to help you understand the tax consequences (disadvantages and advantages) of the options you are considering.
- Alimony can be a source of great dispute and is often symbolic of issues in the divorce. You might argue about alimony when the real problem is that one spouse doesn't feel his or her role as a homemaker has been recognized or one spouse doesn't feel the other was a true financial partner in the marriage. These are important emotions and issues, but you won't resolve them with a check.

alimony is uncertain—it could end tomorrow or on the date agreed upon in your settlement, which may be five years away. If you're the one who is going to receive alimony, you might get all the scheduled monthly payments or only one year's worth if the other person dies. However, a set sum or specific asset that you receive in the property settlement is certain—it's money you get today. When weighing alimony against an asset, you're playing odds. Getting $1,000 a month for three years (if you both live that long) versus $30,000 in cash up front is something to carefully think over. If you like the idea of regular payments but don't like the uncertainty of alimony, you can consider choosing an annuity instead of alimony for part of the property settlement, which brings more certainty.

Health Insurance and Other Expenses

When both of you have been receiving health insurance through one spouse's policy, you will need to make some decisions about coverage after the divorce. Options for the spouse who is not the policyholder include:

- Obtaining coverage through your own employer
- Purchasing an individual policy (or buying it at a group rate through a group such as a local chamber of commerce or other professional association)
- Obtaining coverage through COBRA, a federal law that allows you to stay on your spouse's policy for eighteen months after the divorce if one of you pays the cost of the premiums
- Exploring your eligibility for state income-based health insurance programs

Health insurance and household expenses are items that one spouse may pay for during and/or after the divorce. It is important that you and your spouse and mediator examine the tax consequences of these options before making any decisions because it is important that you are careful about whether you categorize these payments as alimony or property settlement, since there are different consequences for each. Remember that these expenses can be important bargaining chips. Say, "I'm willing to accept a lower alimony payment if you keep me on your health insurance for eighteen months."

Child Support

If you have children, child support must be part of your mediated agreement, or you must present a compelling reason why you have not included it (talk with your mediator about this—it is possible to create an agreement without child support if there are other provisions made for the children's support, but you must meet your state's requirements). The court will carefully scrutinize your agreement when it comes to child support. Child support is paid by the nonresidential parent to the residential parent.

The Purpose of Child Support

Child support is meant to ensure that the children will have the same standard of living as they did prior to the divorce. It is not a punishment, a penalty, a reward, or an affirmation for the parents. Even though child support is meant to be used for the children, there is no requirement that the parent receiving it prove how he or she used the money.

Calculating Child Support

Your mediator will explain to you how child support is calculated, but usually you will need to complete a detailed form that asks information about your income and budget. Each state uses a different form for this, and your mediator will provide you with the form you need to use for your state.

Child support is based on how many children you have and on your and your spouse's income. Your income is calculated, minus FICA. Then a percentage, which is based upon how many children you have (in most states, it is 17 percent for one, 25 percent for two, 29 percent for three, 31 percent for four, and 35 percent for five or more), is applied to this income. You may be able to use other percentages if you provide good reasons.

> **Example:** Juanita and Luis have two children, and Juanita will have residential custody. Juanita's income, minus FICA, is $400 per week. Luis's is $600. Child support is 25 percent in their state. Luis will pay $150 per week in child support.

Note that when you have a true shared parenting agreement, child support may not be necessary or only a small amount may be necessary, but you should discuss this with your attorneys and mediator. Child support does not vary depending on how much time you each spend with your child. If you are the parent paying child support and will spend time with your child on alternate weekends, you can't reduce the amount you pay on those weeks because your child is spending more time at your house. It is a fixed amount that can only be changed by the court. Parenting time is not dependent on child support. A parent cannot be denied time with a child because he or she is late paying child support.

Length of Child Support

Child support ends when the child reaches an age set by your state laws—usually eighteen, nineteen, twenty, or twenty-one—or when the child becomes emancipated (lives independently).

Consequences of Child Support

Child support is not taxable to the person receiving it nor is it tax-deductible for the person paying it. Child support is not a debt that can be discharged in bankruptcy.

▶ *Words That Work* **Talking with Your Spouse About Child Support**

- Child support is important because I need to make sure I have enough money to pay the mortgage and buy food, since both of those things directly relate to Carlos's needs.
- I just don't have room in my budget to pay for all of her dance costumes. Can we work something out?
- Let's see if we can work something out with alimony and child support so that we both get some tax benefits.
- Let's agree to always discuss expenses that come up that have to do with school.
- I understand that child support feels like a double whammy. First, you won't get to see Kaitlyn every day because we agreed she would live at my house. Now, on top of that, the state is saying you have to pay me. I want you to know that I don't think of this as my money. It is money to take care of Kaitlyn's needs.

Mechanics of Child Support

Once you decide how much child support will be paid, you need to consider how it will be paid. Will it be paid weekly, bimonthly, or monthly? Will payment be made directly from one parent to the other, or will payment be made through your state's child support enforcement agency directly from a paycheck? Discuss these options with your spouse and mediator. There are benefits and detriments to each. If payment is made directly from one parent to the other, no one else is involved in your finances; however, if you need help getting late payments from your spouse, it is more complicated. If you use your state child support agency, payments are made directly to the agency and it handles enforcement as well as cost-of-living increases; however, the agency is not forgiving and requires that everything be paid on time in full.

Other Expenses

When you mediate child support, you have the opportunity to think about expenses that are not normally discussed in a divorce settlement. In most states you must spell out who will be responsible for providing health insurance for the child. You may also want to discuss how you will share educational and medical expenses. For example, one spouse may be responsible for all co-pays and deductibles, or you may find a way to share these expenses. And you may need to discuss whether one or both of you will take out life insurance policies with the children as beneficiaries, to provide for their financial support should something happen to one of you. Other child-related expenses you may want to discuss in mediation include:

- College tuition and college savings accounts
- School supplies and expenses, such as field trips, club dues, books, school clothes, SAT preparation classes, tutors, private lessons, registration fees, driver's ed classes, uniforms, equipment, instruments, computers, and more
- Allowances
- Holiday and birthday gifts
- Special occasions, like proms and graduations
- First cars and auto insurance
- Birthday parties
- Weddings
- Bar and bat mitzvahs, first communions, confirmations, or quinceañeras
- Travel to and from parents' homes if it requires air, bus, or train fares

In addition to discussing what expenses are to be paid, discuss how they will be paid. Some parents keep a running tally, assign a percent to each parent, and settle once a year. Others have one parent who pays all expenses for sports while the other pays all expenses for music. You can create any arrangement that works for you.

You also need to discuss a method for payment. You might want to provide each other with written receipts. You might require that some things (such as medical bills) be billed directly to the parent responsible. You might also want to discuss how quickly these types of things will be paid or reimbursed. Talking about details now can help you avoid problems and misunderstandings later.

Tips for Mediating Child Support

- Think in terms of your child's needs. Child support is about making sure your child has a reasonable lifestyle, medical care, and an education.
- Look at accurate incomes and expenses. Be sure to understand what your state considers as income and what is deducted from income before calculating child support.
- Additionally, developing household budgets will help you understand each other's needs, as well as those of your child.
- Be aware that everyone's financial situation is likely to change in the future, and build in the opportunity and methods for renegotiation. You may wish to return to mediation or try to reach an agreement yourselves.
- Think of child support as a benefit that flows from parent to child, not from spouse to spouse.
- Be certain you completely understand your state's child support laws (including provisions like automatic deduction from paychecks and automatic cost-of-living increases, as well as enforcement and collection).
- Remember that child support is separate from property division, alimony, and custody, although mediation offers you the flexibility to think about all of these together as a comprehensive package.
- Think about regular weekly or monthly payments, but also think about expense sharing (such as for educational and

medical expenses) and how you will negotiate future expenses that come up.

- Be aware that child support can be one of the most difficult issues to negotiate because it is a long-term financial commitment that often carries emotional baggage. Be aware when you are negotiating that child support is often symbolic of parental commitment or of a way to get payback for things that happened during the marriage.
- Take a hard look at your budget and what payments will mean to you before agreeing to amounts.
- Make sure you are both completely clear about the legal consequences and procedures that come into play if payments are late.

8

Long Division

Mediating Property Settlements

Frank and Jackie tried to work out a property settlement on their own before going to mediation but were not successful. Frank insisted that he should take the lawn mower, since he was the one who used it. This made no sense to Jackie, since he was moving to a condo and she was staying in their small suburban home. Jackie had only worked part-time so she could take care of the kids and was determined to get a piece of Frank's pension, since she was quite worried about how she would support herself when she was older, but to Frank it was the ultimate insult to have to share the pension he had worked so hard for.

In mediation the mediator encouraged them to each express their opinions and desires. Frank talked about how he had enjoyed tinkering with that lawn mower, how it had come to symbolize his gardening and lawn expertise, and his concerns about how well Jackie would care for it. Eventually it became clear that the mower was important to Frank because of what it represented. Frank and Jackie agreed to sell it and put the proceeds from the sale into the pot of cash they needed to divide. Jackie agreed to pay a neighborhood boy to mow her lawn. This decision respected Frank's attachment to the mower and let him feel as if he were getting some benefit from it.

The mediator then helped them think about retirement. Frank and Jackie were deeply divided when it came to the pension, and they spent an entire session talking about it. Jackie explained that she always felt she really worked a full-time job (being a mom and wife) in addition to her part-time job. The pension represented a reward for all her efforts she had always felt underappreciated for. Frank heard this and told her that her hard work was appreciated and he was grateful for all she had done. The mediator helped them both consider the pros and cons of dividing the pension. Eventually they agreed that Jackie would take a large investment account that she and Frank shared during their marriage and invest it in a conservative way and use that money as her retirement nest egg. This gave Jackie the sense of stability she needed, as well as a feeling that she was being adequately compensated for her role as a supportive spouse all those years. It also gave her the ability to control how the money was going to be invested and paid out. Frank kept his pension, which made him feel that his years of hard work were being respected.

Property settlements lend themselves well to mediation because you have free rein over making decisions based on need; however, it can be a complicated, detailed process—one that a mediator can help you prioritize and organize. Property settlements are not just about dividing up your assets but are about dividing up all of your debts as well.

Getting All the Information

Property settlements are detail oriented, and you must have all the information in place before you can agree on anything. Before you begin to talk about property settlements, your mediator will ask you to gather all the information you need and may ask you to sign something saying that the information you are providing is true, accurate, and complete. The court will insist that you provide complete disclosure to each other about your finances, so this is not a negotiable point.

Understanding the Law

Understanding your state's laws regarding property settlement will give you a good understanding of how a court would make a decision and what kinds of factors would be considered. For many couples, this serves as a guide as to the direction you can take with the settlement, what is fair, and how far you should take a dispute.

Thinking About Property Settlements

Possessions often have emotional meanings, so it's easy to get into a big disagreement about assets when you're really arguing about other issues that have to do with your relationship. The stress and emotion of the divorce can cause you to see things in a clouded way. You may have always hated the vase your spouse's aunt gave you as a wedding gift, but in the course of negotiations, it somehow can become symbolic of all you've gone through and all that you feel has been taken from you. Every once in a while, remind yourself that it really is just stuff. And while stuff can be important, there are other things in life that are more important.

It can also be easy to use stuff to exact revenge or stick it to your spouse. Insisting that your spouse's baseball collection be divided equally when you've really always hated it is a way to hurt the other person. You get nothing of real value out of it other than momentary satisfaction and revenge.

When you're dividing up assets, try to think about what you really need and want. Your lifestyle will probably change after the

115

• • •

> ▶ *Words That Work* **Talking About Property Settlements**

- Let's total up what we think is the real value of our assets before we start dividing things.
- I understand that you would probably use the snowmobile and boat more than I would, but since they are worth so much, I think it is fair then that I keep the rider mower, the gym membership, some cash, and the frequent-flier miles.
- I am uncomfortable sharing my pension with you. Can we think of other ways to compensate for that instead?
- It does sound sensible for you to keep the house, but maybe we should consider the tax consequences of that decision first before we decide.
- Yes, I know you need a couch, but it seems silly to divide up the living room set like that when it is worth more when it's kept together. Let's see if we can find a way for you to get enough money so you can buy a couch.
- I agree that you and the kids need to stay in the house, but if my name stays on the mortgage, it will be impossible for me to buy a place of my own. Are there some other choices we can consider here?

divorce. Think about what kind of life you're going to be living and what kind of things you need to make you comfortable.

Your mediator will help you think about the values of some large assets. Some values are fluid while others are solid. For example, $10,000 in equity in a home is not equal to $10,000 sitting in a savings account. You might not be able to sell the home for as much as you thought, and that equity would just disappear if you had to take a lower sale price (thus this is fluid). When you're making decisions about who gets what, don't forget to take into consideration the solidity of the assets that you are dividing.

In mediation you can think creatively about property settlements. It doesn't have to just be a matter of "you get this, I get that." Instead, you can continue to jointly own things if you wish (such as a vacation home), or you can work out agreements that require long-term payments over time (such as one spouse paying the maintenance fee on a time-share the other spouse will get ownership of).

You must also consider the tax ramifications of the decisions you are making. Capital gains, the increase in value of an asset from the date it was purchased, are taxable. So if one spouse will take over an investment account with a current value of $30,000, but that account was opened for $10,000 and has increased in value, he or she will have $20,000 in taxable capital gains if that account were to be cashed in.

Most people are happy to divide up assets but more reluctant to take ownership of debts. Remember that they go hand in hand, so agreeing to let your spouse have the new car can also mean agreeing he or she is going to be responsible for all the payments.

Understanding Separate Property

Your mediator and attorney will explain to you the difference between separate and marital property and how your state handles these differences. Separate property includes:

- Items and property you owned yourself at the time you got married
- Gifts you received during the marriage, even those from your spouse
- Inheritances you received during the marriage
- Personal injury settlements you received during the marriage

Marital property includes:

- Money earned by either or both of you during the marriage
- Items purchased or obtained during the marriage (this includes concrete things like furniture and cars as well as

nonconcrete things like college degrees or frequent-flier miles)

- The increase in value on separate property items that the other spouse somehow contributed to or helped maintain (such as if your spouse owned rental property and you helped fix it up during the marriage)

Separate property will not be divided in your mediation, but martial property will be. Talk to your attorney or mediator for information about your state's laws.

Property Division Laws

Some states use a community property theory, while others use equitable distribution. In community property states, you each are entitled to half of the marital property, which includes everything acquired during the marriage. In equitable distribution states, the law usually says you have to divide property in a way that is fair, but not necessarily half and half. Your state's laws are an important guideline for you, but in mediation you can divide your property in any way you would like. The only requirement is that it is done in a reasonable way (for example, a settlement where one spouse got everything and the other got nothing would be considered by the court to be patently unfair and unconscionable and would not be approved).

Listing Assets and Debts

One of your homework assignments from your mediator will be to create a complete inventory of your property and debts. This doesn't mean listing every teaspoon, but it does mean listing all large assets and placing an overall value on your total household furnishings. It's a good idea to actually pull out paperwork to get real numbers for property you will be listing. You may have an investment account that you believe is worth about $10,000, but if you pull out the statement you might find it is actually currently worth $9,000 or $11,000. You will also want to get current figures for things like credit card balances, which are always changing. List account numbers and complete names of companies. Go through your list and make sure you have gathered information on all of the following debts and assets:

Debts
- Mortgage
- Home equity loan
- Late rent
- Late taxes
- Past-due utility bills
- Credit card bills
- Personal loans (unsecured loans and loans from relatives)
- Loans against life insurance
- Loans against retirement or pension accounts
- Tuition
- Unpaid health care bills
- Liens against the home
- Merchant accounts (store credit cards)
- Student loans
- Car loans and leases
- Installment payments

Assets
- Real estate
- Vehicles and boats
- Cash value life insurance
- Bank accounts, CDs, and cash
- Retirement and pension accounts, including social security
- Investment accounts, stocks, and bonds
- Licenses and degrees
- Businesses
- Household furnishings and appliances
- Valuable collections and jewelry

- Electronics
- Personal property such as clothing and photographs

You and your spouse can work on creating the list of assets and debts together, or you can do it separately and come to mediation and compare your lists. Either way, you will need to agree about what items are to be listed and what their values are.

Thinking About What You Want

Once you've created a complete list of everything you need to divide, spend some time thinking on your own about how things should be divided. Before you go to the mediation session in which you are going to talk about this, make a list for yourself of the large assets you must have, those you would like to have, and those you don't want. Be sure to put an approximate value next to each item. Then total them at the bottom. (Use the worksheet on the next page.)

Now think about your debts. Divide them into categories: those you definitely should be responsible for, those you might be willing to take responsibility for, and those you don't want to be responsible for. Include the current balance on each one. Then total the columns at the bottom. (Use the worksheet on page 122.)

These lists will give you a starting point when you begin working through these items in mediation.

Property Settlement Approaches

There are different approaches you can take when you mediate property settlements. You can:

- **Be straightforward.** Walk in with your list and put it on the table. Let your spouse know what you consider must-haves and what you are willing to negotiate or give up.

PROPERTY WISH LIST

Must Have	Would Like	Don't Want
Total:	**Total:**	**Total:**

• **Be strategic.** Don't show your list to your spouse and instead focus on negotiation. Tell your spouse that you want the computer and the flat-screen TV even though you're willing to give them up. These items then become your bargaining chips, if you are certain your spouse would want them.

DEBT DIVISION LIST

Definitely Responsible For	Might Be Willing to Be Responsible For	Don't Want to Be Responsible For
Total:	**Total:**	**Total:**

- **Take an in-between approach.** Walk in the door knowing what your bottom line is—what the absolute lowest total value is you will accept (without having a set list of things you have to come away with)—and approach the discussions with a willingness to be flexible on an item-by-item basis.

Your mediator may encourage you to work through property and then debt or vice versa and then look at the bottom line. Or your mediator may suggest that you divide property and the debt that is related to it at the same time (for example, decide at the same time who is getting the car and who is paying the car loan, since they are intertwined).

Dividing Large Assets

There are a variety of large assets you will be dividing. The most common fall in the areas of real estate, retirement accounts, and small business.

Real Estate

When dividing real estate, consider one of the following approaches:

- Sell the property and divide the proceeds, after capital gains are deducted (if any apply—talk to your tax advisor about the laws regarding home sales).
- Continue to jointly own the property (such as a vacation home, which you could take turns using). This is feasible for some people and unthinkable for others.
- Buy each other out. Exchange other assets for one person's share in the home (consider the tax consequences of this, though).
- Continue joint ownership with one spouse making regular "lease-to-own" payments to the other (again, be sure you understand the tax consequences).
- Continue joint ownership and rent the property, using the rent to pay the mortgage and taxes, splitting any profit.

123

If you're going to trade off ownership in the home for other assets, it is important that you get an accurate valuation for the home. A real estate agent can help you do this, or you can pay to have the home appraised. See Chapter 4 for more information.

Retirement Accounts

Talk with your attorney to understand what the rules are for the types of accounts you hold. You will also be able to divide future social security payments in addition to retirement funds that will pay in the future. There are many considerations to take into account when deciding if you want part of your spouse's retirement plan:

- Your ages (and how far away you are from retiring)
- Whether you have your own retirement account
- Whether the plan is vested yet
- How much the account is currently worth
- Whether there will be any distribution to you now
- How well the plan is being managed

When discussing retirement accounts, you must again realize that a bird in hand may be worth two in the bush. The thought of receiving payout when your spouse retires might sound great, but if he or she dies before vesting, you might have been better off to have taken an investment account in the property settlement.

Small Businesses

If one or both of you own a business, you will need to decide how you will get an accurate valuation for the business (see Chapter 4 about using an expert for this). You will need the following documents to determine an accurate value:

- Balance sheet
- Statement of assets and liabilities
- Profit and loss statement
- Income and expense statement

Get an accurate value for the business so you can talk about ways to offset that value to the spouse who will not be the owner. It is possible to continue to co-own a business after divorce, but it is a difficult task because you and your spouse may have trouble working together after divorce. If one of you owned the business before the marriage, you will need to discuss how you will divide the increase in value that occurred during the marriage.

Dividing Debts

It can seem so simple to say, "OK, you'll take the car payment and the loan against life insurance and I'll take the credit cards." Deciding how you want to divide up your debts is one thing, but actually doing it is another. Make sure you talk with your mediator and your spouse about how you are actually going to remove each other's responsibility for debts. In most cases this means refinancing debt or transferring balances to single accounts. And if you want to simply transfer the mortgage to one spouse, you will find that it is almost impossible to do. Again, a refinance may be your only option. Talk with your mediator and attorney about your options and what might work best in your situation.

Dividing Household and Personal Items

Most couples find that they are able to divide much of the smaller household and personal property on their own without assistance, but sometimes specific items can be hotly debated. The best plan is to try to work through these items on your own and then seek your mediator's help with items you can't agree on. It can help to think about dividing things in terms of need. For example, if your spouse is going to rent an apartment that has appliances and you aren't, it makes more sense for the appliances to stay with you. Most children's items usually end up at the home where the children will be spending the majority of their time.

Use these tips to help you divide household items:

- Keep sets together when possible. For example, the china is worth more and is more useful as one set, rather than each of you taking four place settings.

125
. . .

- Be realistic about what you care about, have room for, and can really use. You might love the sleigh bed, but if you don't have room for it, there's no sense in taking it.
- Focus first on use and need, and then worry about equaling out value later.
- Respect the other person's emotional attachments. You might think it's stupid to care about a bobble-head collection, but it might be meaningful to your spouse. Don't insist on dividing or selling something that your spouse has an emotional connection to. You can be compensated for the value of this item by receiving other items in the settlement.
- Don't expect to walk away from this whole, with everything you need for a fully furnished household. You probably are not going to get everything you need and are going to have to buy some essentials yourself.
- Don't take things you don't really want just to make your pile bigger. Instead, create a pile of things neither of you really wants or needs and sell it and split the proceeds, or donate those items to charity and take a deduction on your last joint tax return.

Tips for Mediating Property Settlements

- Don't forget to look at the bottom line (the total amount each person is getting).
- Base decisions on need, not revenge.
- Make deals and negotiate to get the things you want.
- Make sure your children's needs are met.
- Look at all of the circumstances, including alimony, child support, custody, and other factors.

9

Bumps in the Road

Solving Mediation Problems

Joyce and Tim were in their third mediation session and were completely stuck. They could not seem to reach an agreement about the parenting plan. Tim expressed his frustration to the mediator and said that it seemed like mediation was just not going to work for them. Their mediator suggested they each go home and pretend to be the other person. She told them to think about what the other person wanted and why. Then when they came back for the next session, she had them each argue the other person's position. This completely opened their eyes and allowed them to get a real sense of what the other person was feeling. Because they now understood what it was like for the other parent, they were able to work out a plan that took both perspectives into consideration. Tim was certain that if the mediator had not helped them with this exercise, he would have walked away from mediation.

You've covered a lot of bases and learned a lot about cooperation, creativity, and challenges. You and your spouse are dealing with many complicated and emotional issues, but mediation is teaching you that there are ways to find solutions. It's unlikely that you're going to just whiz through mediation and cross the finish line with little or no effort, and sometimes, in the course of mediation, you may come up against a brick wall. When reaching an impasse, many people are compelled to end mediation due to frustration, exhaustion, or anger. Often, though, obstacles are actually an indication that you are about to make a great breakthrough, and everything will suddenly seem to fall into place because mediation is a cumulative process and decisions build on each other.

Although every couple is different and the problems and frustrations they face vary, there are common mediation pitfalls that couples encounter. Do not give up hope. You've invested too much time and energy into mediation to walk away before trying some possible solutions to the most common mediation pitfalls. A good mediator will be prepared for these problems and should be ready to troubleshoot them, if necessary.

Problem: There Is a Lack of Communication

Sometimes one spouse does all the communicating for the couple, and the other is not as responsive or expressive. When you are not equally speaking up and verbalizing your feelings and needs, problems can arise. You aren't a mind reader and can't be expected to know what the other person is thinking or feeling. Sometimes one spouse has difficulty speaking up in mediation and is simply not voicing enough opinions or suggestions.

Solutions

• Tell your mediator and spouse that you are feeling frustrated because your spouse is not responsive enough or communicating enough. It might make you feel as if you are carrying the full burden of mediation or that he or she is not making an effort to participate. Say, "I feel like I'm the only one who is really trying here."

• Instead of jumping in first with your ideas and your solutions, step back and wait for your spouse to go first. Say, "Do you have any thoughts about this?"

- Ask your spouse (or have the mediator ask) what he or she thinks or what he or she can suggest. Say, "Jeff, how do you think we should handle this?"
- Sometimes you get to a point in your relationship where you no longer really hear what the other person is saying. Try to set aside preconceived notions and really listen to what your spouse is saying. Write it down, if that helps you, or try to reword it and say it back ("So what you're saying is . . ."). You may find that there is more to what he or she is saying than you think.
- Don't discount or attack what your spouse says. Of course, you think you're right and can verbalize it quite well, but you're never going to get to an agreement if you're always charging in and ripping apart what the other person is offering.
- Don't put your spouse on the defensive. This will be sure to cause him or her to either go into attack mode or retreat totally, both of which are detrimental to effective communication and mediation.

Problem: There Has Not Been Complete Financial Disclosure

If you suspect that your spouse has not been completely forthcoming with financial information, it can throw a monkey wrench into your mediation. Your suspicions will get the best of you, sooner or later, and block your ability to trust him or her. If your suspicions are correct, you will end up with an agreement that may not be valid (since your state will require full disclosure) or an agreement that ends up not being fair in the long run. If you don't believe you're being told the truth or getting all the details, it's going to be difficult for you to agree to anything for fear of being cheated.

Solutions

- Point out specifically where you feel the information is lacking. A generalized complaint of "you aren't being straight with me" isn't going to get you a solution. Instead, point out exactly what you think is wrong. Obviously, if you don't have the information, you can't say what's missing, but you can point out areas where you believe things have been left out. It can be helpful to point out the reasons why you believe there hasn't been complete disclosure so that it is clear you are not simply making these accusations up.

• Get documentation. If you feel things are being left out, make sure that your proof is in a written document that can be verified by your mediator and/or attorney.

• Get outside help. You may need to have an accountant or a business valuator come into mediation and examine documents.

• If your instincts tell you that disclosure is not complete, listen to those instincts and don't be pushed into an agreement when you just don't feel right about it. If you agree to a financial settlement when you suspect assets are being hidden, you will always be angry and resentful, or you may not receive the closure you need.

• Consult your attorney. If you can't get full disclosure, you can't mediate effectively. Your attorney can help you return to court to legally compel full and complete disclosure.

Problem: You and Your Spouse Can't Agree on the Facts When It Comes to Money

You and your spouse may not be able to agree on certain facts, such as the value of certain assets. You might be sure the house is worth $300,000, while your spouse insists it's only worth a little more than what you paid for it, or you might have total disagreement about the value of the antique rug in your dining room.

Solutions

• Select a neutral third-party evaluator (who is experienced in valuing this type of asset), and agree to use his or her valuation.

• Use one spouse's valuation for one item and the other's for a comparable item.

- Divide everything without resolving the value dispute, and see if you feel the division of property is fair. So, for example, let your spouse take the antique rug even if you can't agree on what it's worth, as long as you are happy with everything you get.

Problem: You Can't Seem to Get Anywhere

If you're at a point in mediation where you're just hitting your heads against a brick wall, going over the same issues and not ever getting anywhere, it can be very frustrating.

Solutions

- Consider taking a break. End a session early or consider canceling the next couple of sessions. Sometimes mediation becomes too intense and you just dread going. There's no rush. You should slow down the pace if it is getting to you. Say, "Maybe we should take next week off so we can think about this."
- Agree that if you can't decide something within a one-hour time frame, you should leave it and return to it later. Say, "We've been at this an hour. Let's give it a rest and come back to it."
- Try to say things in a different way. If you're both sitting in the room repeating the same things over and over, you're not going to make any progress. Think about ways you can reword and restructure what you are saying. Say, "I know I said that I want custody, but what is important to me is that Charles spends most of his time at my house."
- Move on to a different issue. Sometimes if you decide everything else, that one last sticking point suddenly gets cleared up. The air of cooperation spreads, and if you suddenly feel satisfied with everything else, that one last point no longer seems like such a big deal, and you're able to just make a decision.
- Switch roles. Take a few moments and try to argue each other's positions. When you stand in someone else's shoes, you get a much better sense of what they are up against and what they are feeling.

- Ask your mediator to help you see things from your spouse's position. Having someone else reword this for you can be very helpful. Say, "I just do not understand why he wants this. Can you help me understand?"

- Ask your mediator for some suggestions for ways you could settle this problem. Your mediator is not there to find a solution for you, but he or she is supposed to help open your eyes to new considerations and approaches, so don't hesitate to ask for help. Say, "Can you suggest any solutions we haven't thought of yet?"

- Sit down with each other alone outside of mediation and just talk. Talk about other things in your lives or your children. Reconnecting like this can help de-escalate the conflict you're having in mediation.

- Have a brainstorming session. Offer every single solution you can think of to a problem, whether it is good or bad, whether it works for you or doesn't. Say every single solution that comes to mind, and write them all down (your mediator may write these down for you on a flip chart). Don't evaluate or make any judgments about the solutions offered at this point. Just get every single option you can think about listed, then go back and look at them. You may find that one of them works or that one of them suggests a way you can change a previous proposal so that it suddenly works.

- Focus on the needs behind the wants. Instead of getting mad because your spouse wants the house, talk about why he or she wants that and what it means to him or her. If you can understand what you each need and how you emotionally relate to the decisions, you have a better chance of formulating a solution that will work.

Problem: Your Overall Agreement Somehow Seems Unbalanced

Sometimes you move along through mediation and agree to each small decision that is made, but suddenly you look at the big picture and feel as if somehow you're not being treated fairly.

Solutions

- Ask yourself what kind of changes need to be made in order for the agreement to feel fair. Try to pinpoint what is bothering you. For instance, is it financial or is it more to do with your parenting plan?
- Tell your spouse and mediator that you are feeling slighted. Say, "I just don't feel as though this agreement is fair to me, but I can't put my finger on exactly why."
- Make concrete suggestions for ways to tweak things a bit more in your favor.
- Address large changes first, but remember that even small alterations can completely change the way an agreement feels.
- Remind yourself that this is not about coming out a winner but about coming out with a fair and reasonable solution.

Problem: Your Spouse Is Not Cooperating

Sometimes a spouse agrees to mediate but then doesn't follow the rules. Continuous outbursts, unreasonable demands, ultimatums, lies, delays, and accusations can make mediation feel like it has no chance.

Solutions

- Let your mediator try to defuse the situations.
- Ask that your mediator caucus with each of you to get to the root of the problems (see Chapter 3). Say, "Could we maybe talk to you separately about this?"
- Suggest shuttle mediation, so you don't have to witness your spouse's outbursts (see Chapter 1).
- Create deadlines or concrete boundaries. Listen to your spouse's dialogues for three minutes at a time before stepping in and saying it is now your turn to speak for three minutes. Or be very clear and say that you will not engage in a discussion when your spouse becomes angry or yells. Your mediator should be able to help you set up rules for behavior and then enforce them.
- Talk to your attorney and create an exit strategy, so if you decide to end mediation, you will have a game plan. If you aren't

able to move past your spouse's rage or refusal to cooperate, find out how quickly your attorney can file papers and get the court process moving.

Problem: You Decide You Don't Like Your Mediator

There might come a time in mediation when it suddenly hits you that you just don't like, don't trust, or don't feel comfortable with your mediator.

Solutions

• Look at what it is you don't like. Is it personal? Is it a trust issue? Or is it a communication issue? Just because you decide this isn't a person you want to be pals with does not mean that he or she is a person you can no longer work with or someone who isn't a good mediator.

• Express your concerns. Maybe you feel as if the mediator is biased somehow or has said something that hurt your feelings. There may have been a misunderstanding, but you'll never resolve it if you don't get it out in the open. Say, "OK, right now I'm feeling like you are completely siding with her."

• Think about whether it is the mediator or the process you dislike. It is easy to transfer your feelings about mediation to the mediator. Separate out concerns about the process from the mediator. Think about whether you could continue if you were working with a different mediator or if things about the process were changed. If the answer is yes, then mediation is still an option for you.

• You can end mediation and find a new mediator if you feel your differences are that severe or you feel that the process is not working. Explain to your spouse that you are committed to the process and would like to continue but can only do so with a new mediator. Involve your spouse in finding a new mediator.

• End mediation and choose collaborative law or go to court.

• Ask yourself if you are just feeling uncomfortable talking about personal issues. Some people find it hard to accept the mediator's suggestions or answer his or her questions. This doesn't mean your mediator is not doing a good job, but it may mean you are not yet fully open to the process.

Problem: You Don't Want to Do the Homework

"Homework? You've got to be kidding!" This might be your reaction when you learn you are going to be given assignments to complete outside of mediation. Some people are resistant to the idea of doing this work.

Solutions

• Find out what purpose the homework serves. If your mediator explains why certain assignments are important and what they are going to do for you, you may feel better about doing them. Say, "So what is the reason for this homework?"

• Realize the cost savings. Homework allows you to gather information and documents on your own time, instead of wasting mediation time, saving you money in the long run.

• Understand that much of this homework has to be done no matter what. This kind of work is not unique to mediation at all. Whether you go through the courts or through a mediator, divorce requires that you organize financial paperwork and work out a budget and figure out how to divide it all up. Even if you have your attorney handle your divorce, it will still be your responsibility to do this work.

135

• • •

Problem: You Have No Idea What Is Reasonable

It can be difficult to know what is reasonable in a divorce settlement, particularly if you have never been divorced before and have no close friends or family who are divorced.

Solutions

- Talk to your attorney. Go over the issues and ask for guidance as to what would be reasonable settlements for each, based on court precedents as well as his or her opinion and experience.
- Pay attention to what will work for your family. If something is a reasonable settlement for 90 percent of the population, that doesn't necessarily mean it will work for your family. Link solutions to your family's needs, not to the consensus.
- Listen to your gut instinct. If it feels unreasonable, it probably is unreasonable. Go with your gut and give yourself time to sit with whatever is bothering you. Sleep on it, write it down, or talk to your mediator. Don't respond hastily, but if you think it over and something just doesn't feel right, you have to trust yourself.

Problem: You Encounter a Big Problem Outside of a Mediation Session

Because your lives are in flux and you have to deal with each other in real life and not just in the mediation room, it's likely that you might encounter a problem and have a disagreement about it outside of mediation. For example, you might have a blowup over a change in the parenting plan, an argument about who should get to keep the car, or a disagreement about who took the power drill.

Solutions

- Don't revert to old patterns. When you were living together, you had a way of dealing with problems that may not have been very productive. If you're standing in the home you lived in together, it can be easy to just slip back into the comfortable roles that you had when you were together. You're learning a new way to relate to each other now, though, so it's important to break the old patterns.
- Use your mediation skills to approach this problem. Listen to each other, create solutions, and try to find one that you both can live with. This may mean you each have to give in a little, and in the heat of the moment, that can be hard to do.

• If a permanent solution is not forthcoming, work out a temporary one. Say, "Yes, you can have the kids this weekend, but we need to sit down and figure out how to compensate for that so they have time with me as well."

• If possible, put it on hold. Say, "I think we should wait and talk about this with the mediator." Schedule an emergency mediation session, or save it for your next session. Working through the problem in the mediation session may help you look at it more calmly and find workable solutions.

Problem: You Reached an Agreement, but One of You Broke It

Because your agreement is an evolving creature and because you often can't know if something works until you try it, there are times when one of you may break an agreement.

Solutions

• Find out or explain why the agreement was broken. If you can find out what went wrong, you have a better chance of fixing it. Say, "I didn't think about the fact that we agreed we would talk to each other before making plans for the kids on the weekend. The birthday party invitation came and I just said yes."

• Don't lie. If you're the one who broke the agreement, don't lie about it. Whether you had a legitimate reason or not, you aren't going to be able to lie and move on with mediation as if this didn't happen. Say, "You're right, I did take the money."

• Consider if the agreement still works. Often an agreement is broken because it was flawed. For some reason it wasn't quite right for your situation. Figure out if any parts of it still work. If nothing can be salvaged, approach the problem again and look for other solutions.

• Get anger in check. Of course, you're going to be ticked off if your spouse doesn't hold up his or her end of the bargain. Register your disappointment, betrayal, and hurt. Then you've got to pick yourself up and start working on a solution.

- Find out if this failure is linked to other problems. There may be a whole structure of agreements that are linked together, and once one fails, the others are going to tip over like a row of dominoes. Fix all related issues. For instance, if you're having trouble paying your bills right now, it's likely you're not going to be able to swing the child support payments either.

Problem: Your Spouse Makes Last-Minute Changes or Demands

Sometimes you think you've just about got something nailed down, and the mediator reviews it with you one last time—and then your spouse suddenly speaks up and wants a change or asks for more of something. It can be frustrating to get to the finish line and then be stopped in your tracks like this.

Solutions

- Find out what the problem is. Sometimes things seem right in theory, but when the logistics are in place, doubt can take over. Get details about what your spouse is objecting to so that you can work through the problem. Say, "So what exactly is it about the parenting schedule that is bothering you? Is it the frequency, the pickup times, or the dates we picked?"
- Review your agreement in detail. An objection can come up because your spouse is feeling overwhelmed by the big picture. When you walk through the agreement piece by piece and your spouse can see again that he or she did agree to each small part, things won't feel so large and overwhelming.
- Remember that it is better to make changes now than to finalize your agreement and have it not work. If there are problems, you want to deal with them now and not sometime in the future, when mediation is over and you're trying to get on with your life. Say, "I am not trying to hold things up here, but it's important to me that we get this completely right so we don't have problems with it down the road."

- Don't throw in the towel. It's easy to get upset at this turn of events and trash the whole thing. You've come so far and worked through so many things that it doesn't make sense to give up now.
- Be aware of negotiating tactics. Sometimes if you wait until something is almost resolved and throw in another demand, the other person might agree to it just to get things over with. This might be a tactic your spouse is taking. Resist the urge to give in just to get the process over with. Keeping track along the way of what the sticking points were and noticing if any are resurfacing can be helpful.

Problem: You Just Feel Uneasy About Mediation

Sometimes people feel unsure about the mediation process, even if they didn't at the beginning. It's one thing to agree that you'll talk to your spouse, think up solutions, and make compromises, but it's another thing to actually do all that.

Solutions
- Face your fear. What are you afraid of? Is it a loss of control? Is it a fear of financial independence? Does it have something to do with parenting? There is an underlying worry that is getting to you, and unless you uncover it and deal with it, you're not going to get anywhere.
- Get help when you need it. If you're feeling overwhelmed in mediation, ask for help. Tell your mediator how you're feeling. Talk to your attorney. Explore the possibility of bringing someone with you to mediation, such as your attorney or some kind of support person. Talk about your feelings with a therapist.
- Take a wait-and-see attitude. Even if can't gauge how much progress you are making in mediation, keep working at it. Mediation is a learned skill, and you may need a while to really learn how to do it. You're going to be wobbly when you get started, but your mediator is there to guide you along.

> ▶ *Words That Work* Ways to Talk Through
>   Mediation Problems

- I am just not seeing a solution to this problem. Maybe we should move on to something else and come back to this.
- I don't feel like my opinion is being considered. Could we stop a minute and talk about what I am suggesting?
- I'm sorry, I don't think I was very clear. What I was suggesting was this. . . .
- I am feeling really angry/upset right now. I need to end the session and try another day.
- I know you want to take the kids on Christmas, but I do, too. We have to stop arguing about this now. We should take a break from this issue now and talk about it at our next mediation session.
- I really don't understand how this whole tax thing works. And I can't agree to it until I do. Can we go over it again in a different way?
- I am feeling really frustrated that you aren't trying to offer any solutions. All you're doing is sitting there shooting down everything the mediator and I suggest.
- This is what we agreed to, and you didn't follow our agreement. I don't think we should argue about it, but w e should find a way to change it or fix it so it will work for us. Can you explain what part of it is not working for you?
- Yes, I understand what you're proposing, but I absolutely have no idea if that is a fair amount for alimony. I need to talk to my lawyer to see what he thinks before I agree to anything.

Problem: You Can't Stand Up for Yourself

You might reach a point where you feel like you're not standing up for yourself in mediation. Maybe you're letting your spouse steam-roll you into things you aren't comfortable with, or maybe you're steamrolling yourself into things because you just want it to be over. You might still be looking for approval from your spouse.

Solutions
- Revisit issues. Even if you have already agreed to something but now realize you were pushed into it, go back to that issue in mediation and look at it again.
- Look at the mediator, not your spouse, when you talk. If you're feeling pressured or unable to speak for yourself, looking at the mediator may be less threatening than looking at your spouse. Direct your comments to the mediator if it helps you.
- Express your frustration to the mediator. The mediator can help you stand up for yourself by asking your opinion and encouraging you to offer responses and suggestions. He or she may also suggest caucusing or shuttle mediation.
- Don't agree to anything without fully talking it through. It can be easy to just jump on board the first solution offered. Instead, really explore all the options available, and don't agree to one unless you really think you can live with it.

Problem: You Just Don't Know What You Want

Sometimes you might not know what you want to do or are unsure about the direction in which you'd like to see each issue go.

Solutions
- Move on to another topic. Moving on to something else will give you the time you need to work through a problem. Also, once you make other decisions, they may clearly point the way for how this decision should be made.
- Ask that some more options be generated. You might be undecided simply because none of the choices you are confronted with really work for you.
- Get input. Talk to friends and family and your attorney to get some input on the issue at hand and advice on where to go with it.

Ending Mediation

It is your right to end mediation if it is not working for you or you are not comfortable with it. If you or your spouse chooses to end mediation, see if you can't at least get a written agreement for the decisions you've already made. You've invested a lot of time and money into mediation, so you should try to walk away with something substantial. A partial agreement will cut down on future attorney costs and speed up your court process.

Don't feel bad if mediation doesn't work out for you in the long run. The most important thing is to have your divorce handled in a way that makes you comfortable and helps make sure your needs are completely met.

Tips for Solving Mediation Problems

- Stay calm and remember that every couple in mediation encounters difficult problems.
- Don't blame your spouse as the cause of the problem. You're in this together, and you must find a solution together.
- Be patient. Solutions are not always immediately obvious and are only found after spending time considering all the options.
- Take time to deal with emotions. You can't move forward until you're emotionally ready.
- Ask your mediator for suggestions and options. He or she may see choices you don't.

10

Closing the Book

Finalizing Your Divorce

Tanya and Jim had worked through mediation and now had to decide how they were going to finalize their divorce in the courts. Their state did not have no-fault divorce, so one of them was going to have to file papers with the court essentially blaming the other for the end of the marriage. Tanya was horrified at the thought of this and simply felt sick that one of them had to put in writing bad things about the other. Tanya and Jim's mediator explained to them that this was just a legal requirement and it did not have to mean they really wanted to blame the other person. They discussed the various possibilities and agreed to use cruel and inhuman treatment as the grounds for their divorce, since it was a very loose catchall statement in their state. Jim had a higher income than Tanya and offered to file the papers and be the plaintiff, but Tanya could not bear the thought of a judge deciding that she was the one who had caused the marriage to end, so they agreed that she would be the plaintiff and Jim would reimburse her for the court and legal fees.

Once they decided that, they had to figure out some details of how they would implement their settlement and worked out a plan for transferring debt, closing accounts, and dividing their household belongings. They signed the agreement after consulting with their attorneys.

Tanya and Jim also held a closure ceremony at their last mediation session, where they simply took a few moments alone to say good-bye and thank each other for the good times. They shook hands and each cried a little. When she left the office, Tanya felt as if a weight had been lifted from her shoulders.

You've covered a lot of ground and laid a new foundation for many aspects of your new life separate from your spouse. You've worked out or begun to work out property settlements, alimony, child support, and a parenting plan. But closing the door on your marriage is as much an emotional step as it is financial and personal. The mediation process can help you obtain the closure you need to move forward. Traditional divorce sends you into court, where you openly discuss each other's faults, and then hands you a piece of paper and sends you on your way. You're never given an opportunity to process the ending of the marriage or to create an exit strategy. Mediation offers you the opportunity to come to a gradual ending, a kind of de-escalation of your marriage. You slowly work through all the decisions and implement them as you need to, you decide exactly how you will proceed with the divorce and legal paperwork, and then, if you wish, you can create a formal ending to the marriage, which can give you that feeling of closure you need.

Formally Ending Your Marriage

One of the choices you will need to make will be how you will legally end your marriage. There are different ways to go about this, depending on your state laws and your personal situation.

Divorce

Each state has different rules and procedures for divorces. The biggest decision you will need to make is the legal reason you give for the end of your marriage.

Your state may have a no-fault divorce process, in which you mutually agree that your marriage is not working, wait a certain period of time, and end it without pointing fingers. In some states you can file for a separation, which is then converted to a divorce, using the separation as the reason for the divorce after a certain period of time. This may be an avenue to consider if your state does not have no-fault divorce, since it does not require you to blame each other.

If your state does not allow no-fault divorce, you need to choose from your state's grounds (legal reasons) for divorce and select the one that will work in your situation. Grounds for divorce can

▶ *Words That Work* **Legally Ending Your Marriage**

Consider these words to help you talk about ways to finalize your divorce:

- Since I moved out of the home, I will agree it was legal abandonment as long as we both understand I would never abandon my children or my responsibility to them.
- I think we can both agree we called each other names and provoked arguments and that this happened on at least three separate occasions. Since the mediator says that is our state's definition of cruel and inhuman treatment, I will agree to it.
- We both know we both played some role in the downfall of this marriage, but I really don't think fault is what we should be concerned about here. Let's not point fingers and just agree to use whatever grounds for divorce is simplest. We will both know in our hearts that it was a mutual decision.

145

include adultery, imprisonment, or mental incompetence, but in mediation most couples select abandonment, cruel and inhuman treatment, or legal separation as grounds. Talk with your mediator and attorney about your state's requirements and what will work best for you. Again, remember that these are just legal words and you do not have to completely agree with their tone.

One person will need to file papers with the court to begin the divorce; this is the plaintiff, the person who is officially asking for the divorce. The other spouse is the defendant. In mediation you will decide who will be the plaintiff and who will be the defendant. This decision is important for court purposes but does not have to have an emotional impact on you personally. If you decide together how the divorce is going to proceed, you are both in control and both managing it. Often the spouse with more financial resources is the one who becomes the plaintiff, but you and your spouse can make any arrangement that works for you.

The plaintiff is normally responsible for:

- His or her own legal fees
- Court filing fees
- Court transcription fees
- Fee for legal process service

In mediation, though, you can negotiate financial responsibility for any costs of the legal divorce.

146

Separation

You can submit a separation agreement to the court, which puts into place all of the decisions you made in mediation, without formally ending your marriage. This is an option for you on a temporary basis or on a long-term basis. Some couples feel that by completing mediation they have truly ended their marriage in every way that matters to them and don't need the state to agree with them. If this is an option you are considering, consult with your attorney about the effect on social security, taxes, and inheritance.

Annulment

In some circumstances, couples can legally annul a marriage, but this is unusual in mediation, since annulments are most common for very short marriages (and a short marriage usually does not involve a lot of decisions that need to be mediated). An annulment is a legal determination (religious annulments are different) that your marriage was not valid from the beginning. Annulment may be available as a legal option if any of the following are true:

- One of you was underage at the time of marriage.
- One of you misrepresented yourself to the other in some significant way.
- One of you was mentally ill.
- One of you was unable to or unwilling to consummate the marriage.
- One of you concealed important facts, such as having a disease or previous children.

An annulment has almost the same legal effect as divorce, allowing you to divide property and determine custody (children born to the marriage are still considered legitimate even if an annulment is granted). The only difference is the court says that the marriage was never truly valid from the beginning.

Reviewing Your Final Written Agreement in Mediation

147

Once you have completely mediated your agreement, your mediator will put it in writing. He or she may then mail it to you or give it to you at a session. You will most likely then meet with your spouse and mediator and go over the provisions of the agreement in detail and make sure it contains everything you agreed to. Pay careful attention to the document and make sure you understand and agree with everything it says. Compare this document to the notes you have made on your mediation checklist. If you have any questions, second thoughts, uncertainty, or confusion, you must speak up. Ask your attorney to review the agreement at this point. While this document may not be a formal legal document, it can be used as evidence of an agreement, so it is important that you only sign it once you are certain you agree with it.

Your mediator may ask you to sign a memorandum of understanding (a formal written description of your agreements, but not a court document), which will be sent to your attorneys for conversion into a legal document. The memorandum of understanding is not legally binding in court, but it is a clear indication that you've come to an agreement and allows your attorneys to simply lift the language out and place it into the necessary court documents. The attorney representing the person who will be the plaintiff will file the court papers. If you are working with an attorney-mediator, he or she may be able to create the actual legal document your attorney will file with the court. An attorney-mediator will most likely have you read and verbally agree to the document and then send it to your attorneys for their review. Once your lawyers approve the document, you will sign it.

What to Look for in an Agreement
Your agreement should be complete and clear and should include the following provisions or sections:

- **Description of the parties.** Your names, social security numbers, dates of birth, date and place of marriage, and addresses must be provided, as well as a listing of the attorneys representing you. You may need to specify the date when you physically separated.
- **Termination of the marriage.** You agree to a legal reason (grounds) for the divorce, and the person who will take the agreement to court is specified (see earlier in this chapter). If your state requires a legal separation first or if there is a waiting period, be sure that is specified as well.
- **Fees.** If you have an agreement about sharing attorney fees or paying costs, this must be included.

- **Parenting.** Names and dates of birth of the children should be listed. Your parenting plan should be laid out in detail, explaining custody and visitation. If you have agreed to have mutual access to health and education records, make sure that this is stated.
- **Child support.** The agreement should list the child support payments, how often they are to be paid, their amounts, and when child support will end. If payment will be by income deduction, this must be specified. If you are not following your state's guidelines, the agreement must note this and explain why. If you have agreed on expense sharing or certain expenses to be paid or reimbursed by one parent, this must be specified.
- **Health insurance.** If one parent will provide health insurance for the child, this needs to be stated. If you have an agreement about one spouse paying for the other's health insurance, this should be explained. If one or both parents will take out a life insurance policy that benefits the children, this should be specified.
- **Alimony.** If you have agreed on alimony, the amounts and frequency must be listed, as well as the termination date and the reason for alimony.
- **Property agreement.** Verify that all marital debts are listed and distributed. Check that all financial assets and property are listed and distributed. Go over the list of household or personal items that have been divided. Make sure any intangible assets have been included.
- **Taxes.** Check that the agreement specifies who will list any children as dependents. If you have an agreement about a tax refund or debt, make sure that is spelled out.
- **Religious annulment.** If you have agreed to cooperate with a religious annulment process now or in the future, make sure that is included.
- **Complete agreement.** The agreement should state that it is the complete agreement and that nothing is left out.
- **Agreement to mediate.** If you've agreed to use mediation instead of returning to court to resolve any future problems, this must be included. This clause might say that you agree to attempt mediation for a "reasonable period of time" or for a set number of sessions before going to court.

- **Names.** Most agreements specify that both parties will have the right to revert to using a premarital name, whether or not you intend to do so at this time.
- **Other agreements.** If you have children, you have probably made other agreements in mediation (about things such as children's laundry, discussing large gifts, coordinating rules, and so on) to help you parent together more effectively. Your mediator will most likely include these rules in the memorandum of understanding, but in many states these are not issues the court will get involved in, so your attorneys may choose to not include these agreements in your court papers. While you cannot legally compel each other to follow agreements that are not formalized by the court, your mediator should impress upon both of you the importance of honoring your agreement and parenting cooperatively. You will need to sign a statement at some point that the agreement you are submitting to the court is your complete agreement, but practically speaking, many couples have other informal agreements with each other that are not written into their divorce papers.

Second Thoughts About Your Agreement?

Sometimes when you see something in writing it suddenly seems different or takes on a different meaning than when you are simply discussing it. Additionally, when you see all of your agreements written down in detail, they can seem overwhelming. You may have doubts, be nervous, or be uncertain once you've read the entire agreement. This happens to a lot of people, so don't panic. If you are experiencing any of these feelings, set up another session in which you can talk about them, ask for time to think it over, or point out problems at the session in which the mediator gives you the agreement.

Your mediator should take your concerns seriously. If your spouse becomes upset or impatient, remind him or her that you want to make sure the agreement is accurate and that you understand it. You both have put a lot of work into this and want to make sure it is exactly right.

▶ *Words That Work* **Problems with the Agreement**

Use these lines to help you express your concerns about the agreement:

- Can you explain to me exactly what item number 6 means? I remember discussing it, but I just am not sure that this is what we agreed to.
- When I look at this overall agreement, it just doesn't feel fair to me. Here are the reasons. . . .
- I need some time to read this over and think about it. Can we set up another time to talk about any questions we might have?
- I'm not trying to be difficult, but I'm pretty sure this is not what we agreed to exactly for child support. Let me explain. . . .
- I need some help digesting this. I'd like to talk to my attorney and then meet again.
- I understand what item number 3 means, but I am just not comfortable with the way it is worded. Is there another way to say this that might put me at ease?

Consulting with Your Attorney

After you have met with your mediator and made sure the agreement is complete, you will need to meet with your separate attorneys. Your attorney will want to make sure that you agreed to everything in the document and that nothing is left out. He or she may want to go over legal or technical details with you about filing or specific legal clauses that will be included in your court papers. If you have any questions or concerns about the agreement or the legal documents the attorneys will create, bring them up now.

One of the attorneys will then create the final legal documents that will be filed with the court, and both of you will need to sign them. Your attorney will go over this document with you in detail

> **Tips for Finalizing Your Agreement**
>
> - Compare the document to the notes you have made on your mediation checklist.
> - Take the time to read the entire agreement thoroughly and carefully.
> - Ask about things that you do not understand.
> - Check with your attorney before signing anything you are unsure about.
> - Consider each clause of the agreement first, and then move on to reviewing it as a whole.

before you sign it, and, again, if you have any questions or concerns, bring them up.

Court Procedure

Once the document has been signed and filed with the court, you may have a waiting period before it is accepted and your divorce decree is issued. You may also need to appear in court and testify. If you need to do this, your attorney will discuss this with you and tell you how many appearances are required and what is involved in your state. If you are required to testify, the appearance will be brief and no one will be cross-examining you. Usually testimony is required to ensure you agreed to the document and that the facts in it are true.

Obtaining Closure

Finalizing the written agreement is one aspect of obtaining closure on your marriage, but in reality, there will still probably be some issues you need to work through before things can truly be over.

Financial Closure

Although your mediated agreement will lay out all of the financial decisions you've made, you will still need to find a way to implement them as easily and efficiently as possible. You may need to mediate the following decisions:

- When one of you will move out of the marital home
- When you will give back keys to homes or vehicles (you could exchange these at a final mediation session)
- When you will close credit card accounts or transfer balances
- When you will empty or close a safe deposit box
- When you will close bank accounts (make sure all checks have cleared before doing so)
- When you will close or transfer investment accounts
- When you will roll over or move retirement accounts (you will need to wait for special paperwork from your attorneys to do this)
- When and how you will divide up household property (for some couples it is easiest if one person comes and takes things while the other spouse is away, whereas other people want to be present to see the actual division taking place; see Chapter 8 for more information)
- When you will change the payee's name on utility bills for a home only one of you will remain in
- When loans will be paid off or transferred
- When child support payments or alimony payments will begin and what kind of process you will use—check, cash, paycheck deduction—as well as whether receipts will be regularly issued
- When title and deed changes will be made to vehicles and real estate

Spiritual Closure

If a religious annulment is an option, discuss if either of you is interested in pursuing it. If so, you will probably want your agreement to specify that you both agree to cooperate with the proceedings required by your church (some states require that all divorce judgments specify this). Religious annulments can be important if one or both of you hope to someday remarry in the church. Note that even if you obtain a legal annulment from your state, it is not the same thing as an annulment from your church. To learn more about religious annulment criteria and procedures, as well as whether an annulment would benefit you, talk to your clergy or religious leader.

Emotional Closure

Many people find that although mediation has allowed them to fairly and amicably end a marriage, they still walk away without the proper tools to adjust to their new lives and move on. Obtaining emotional closure is one of the most important and difficult steps you can take in mediation.

Emotional closure brings you full circle in mediation. You and your spouse completely tie up all loose ends and walk away from the process knowing that you have fully and completely resolved

---

▶ *Words That Work* Emotional Closure

Here are some ways to say good-bye as you create closure:

- Thank you for helping me create and raise our wonderful children.
- We had some good times, didn't we? Let's try to remember those instead of the bad ones.
- I really hope you find happiness and peace, and I wish you only good things.
- We entered our marriage with hope. Let's end it with hope for our separate futures.
- I want to apologize for things I have done that have hurt you.

all of the issues that are between you. There are several methods for obtaining emotional closure.

Using Therapy

Attending couples therapy is a way to obtain emotional closure. You can express your emotions to each other, find a way to say good-bye, and discover confidence in yourselves to live separately. You may find that individual therapy works better for you. Working through your feelings with a good therapist can provide an excellent outlet and a good way to resolve lingering issues from the divorce.

Closure Ceremonies

Because mediation is such a flexible process, you can do anything you need to get you through the divorce process. Some couples feel the need for a formal closure ceremony, which is meant to undo the wedding ceremony and bring a formal end to their marriage. If this is something you are interested in, discuss this option with your mediator and consider the following possibilities for closure ceremonies:

- Saying a formal good-bye to each other at your last mediation ceremony with a handshake or a hug
- Formally signing the mediation agreement as you did the wedding license
- Burning a copy of your marriage license (don't burn the original)
- Reversing the unity candle ceremony—lighting two separate candles from one large one and then blowing out the large one
- Promising to work together as parents
- Taking time to thank each other for the good things you've shared and forgive each other for mistakes and bad feelings
- Exchanging meaningful items, like giving back wedding bands, splitting up a stack of photos, or giving back the key to the marital home

155

Tips for Finding True Closure

- Begin a new life for yourself and explore new interests and new experiences.
- Rely on family and friends to help you through difficult times.
- Realize that it will take time to fully and completely accept what has happened and heal.
- Find a way to forgive your spouse for what he or she has done in the marriage.
- Choose to forgive yourself for what you have done in the marriage.
- Realize that you can't erase your marriage but you can get over the hurt it may have caused you.

Facing the Future

Dealing with Problems After Divorce

Krista and Taylor were divorced at last. When the divorce decree came in the mail, Krista felt like it was finally all over. She slowly began to realize, though, that she and Taylor were going to have lots of contact with each because of their children. Even though they had a detailed parenting plan, it seemed like things were always coming up that made it necessary for them to talk to each other and make decisions. Krista found herself falling back into old patterns when she talked to Taylor. She would still ignore his opinions, overreact when he offered alternatives, and feel very defensive. Krista's friend reminded her that she and Taylor had been able to work things out in mediation, so maybe she should try using her mediation skills when she talked to Taylor. This took some mental adjustment, but soon Krista found she was able to approach situations with Taylor as she had in mediation. She remained calm, asked questions, looked for solutions, and presented alternatives. Before long she found that they were able to resolve many problems with little turmoil.

Once mediation has ended you probably will give a big sigh of relief. You've signed your agreement and begun the court process to formalize it. You're beginning your new life. It's not going to be all roses and sunshine, however. Even though the heavy lifting is behind you, you still have some things to work out.

Rules for the Future

Your mediator might have helped you work out some ground rules for how you will deal with each other in the future. If not, it's time to set some up. You can do this on your own, or you can meet with your mediator if you need help.

Parenting Rules

If you have children, it is likely your mediator will have encouraged you to talk and think about future issues. Some things to consider are:

- When you will introduce children to dates or new partners
- Whether adult overnight guests will be part of your lifestyle when your children are at your home
- How you will negotiate changes to the parenting plan
- When you will create a holiday and vacation schedule each year
- How you will discuss and consider new parenting expenses that come up
- What you will do if one of you wishes to move away
- Whether you will refrain from saying negative things about the other parent in front of your child

Other Rules

If you do not have children, rules for the future may not have been something you discussed in mediation. Even though you're getting divorced and you don't have kids, you aren't completely free of each other. You still have business to take care of. You may need to:

- Divide up personal property
- Make payments to each other as part of the property settlement
- Close accounts and pay off debts
- Pay or receive alimony
- See each other in social or business settings
- Share mutual friends
- Share a pet
- Wait for a home to sell

It is important to set up some rules for how you will deal with each other in these situations. Sample rules might include:

- Alimony payments will be mailed on the first of each month, and a receipt will be mailed back the day after it is received.
- You will not pump mutual friends for information about each other.
- You will take one specific day and go through all remaining personal property that needs to be divided.
- If you are sharing time with a dog, you will meet in a park to exchange the dog.
- You will transfer balances out of joint credit cards by the end of the month and then officially close the accounts.

159

. . .

Mediating Postdivorce Conflict on Your Own

If you're experiencing conflict, you might want to try self-mediation before coming back to mediation to resolve your post-divorce issues. Think back to the rules and procedures you followed when you were in mediation, and try to replicate them on your own. This may help you resolve some of the smaller or

Tips for Successful Self-Mediation

- Create ground rules that you will follow while attempting to self-mediate. These can include no raised voices, accusations, discussion of relationship issues, or emotional outbursts.
- Plan scheduled sessions of set duration to work on the issues.
- Meet in a comfortable and neutral place.
- Tackle only one issue at a time.
- Take turns offering possible solutions.
- Listen to each other's solutions with an open mind.
- Take breaks if needed.
- Write down things you agree on.
- Table issues you can't seem to resolve and come back to them.
- Provide each other with complete information and disclosure.
- Focus on finding solutions, not on finger-pointing or revenge.
- If you're having trouble staying on point, consider asking a mutual friend to sit with you and help you try to reach some agreements.

easier issues and reduce the actual time you might need to spend with a mediator.

Self-mediation can be very effective, and even if you can't work out all of the issues, you can probably work out at least some, thus decreasing the time and expense if you do hire a lawyer or mediator. There's no magic wand a mediator waves that makes your case easy to settle. It is simply a matter of taking a solution-oriented approach to the things you need to decide.

If you do use self-mediation, be sure to write down what you agree to so that there is no question to what will be part of your agreement. This will also make it easy for your lawyer or mediator to process your agreement into a legal document.

Mediating After Divorce

You probably see the finalization of your divorce as closing the book on your problems with your spouse. Unfortunately in many families, that's not the case. If you didn't understand each other and couldn't agree before the divorce, it's likely that you still won't afterward, even if you've gone through mediation to get a divorce. Mediation can provide solutions for many issues and conflicts that come up after the divorce and can help you avoid having to go to family court to deal with custody or child support issues.

If you return to mediation after divorce, though you understand the process and have some experience with it, you might find that you really need to go back to get some help ironing out the problems you've encountered. The first choice you will need to make is whether you will use the same mediator.

▶ *Words That Work* Postdivorce Discussions

Use these sentences to you help you with your postdivorce discussions:

- Why don't you explain the reasons behind your position so that I can understand it better.
- I think we both agree on X and Y and just need to figure out an answer that will work for us on Z.
- Let's see if we can think of some other solutions that may not have occurred to us earlier.
- I totally understand your point of view. You're saying X.
- I would like to find a solution that we can both feel comfortable with.
- I think maybe we should both take a little time to consider the options we've discussed and see if a solution comes to us. I know I could use a break.

You should not return to the same mediator and should seek out a new one if any of the following are true:

- One of you felt the process was biased in some way.
- One of you felt strong-armed into a settlement.
- You felt the process took too long.
- The location is no longer convenient for both of you.

Mediation is not a choice for you and you should consult an attorney if:

- Family violence has become an issue.
- Drug or alcohol use has become an issue.
- Child abuse has become an issue.

When you return to mediation, it is key that you spell out for the mediator what the problems are that you are confronting. And since you both may not agree about what those problems are, you will each need to offer your own version or explanation.

Issues you might bring to postdivorce mediation include:

- One of you wants to change custody.
- One of you wants to change the visitation schedule.
- The custodial parent wants to relocate.
- One of you wants to increase or decrease child support.
- You disagree about how to share medical or educational expenses for your child.
- You disagree about a medical or an educational decision involving your child.
- Alimony or child support has not been paid, and you need to negotiate how to make up lost payments and make sure future payments are made.
- A problem has come up with your property settlement.

Postdivorce mediation is a bit different from divorce mediation. When you mediate a divorce, the mediator has a list of issues and decisions you need to make. But when you return to mediation after divorce, you have to lay the framework for the decisions, so you are in charge of setting the agenda. And very often there are relevant issues lurking beneath the surface of your particular conflict that will need to be brought out in order to find a solution. Your mediator will recognize this and help you look at:

- Things that have caused or been impacted by this problem or disagreement
- Rules you have been following (or breaking) and whether they are effective
- Changes in each of your lives and changes you are contemplating
- Changes in your children's lives and needs
- How your relationship with each other has changed and in what direction you need it to change

Most cases of postdivorce mediation can be handled in two to three sessions. Some couples can even resolve things in one session. In general, your mediator will want to hear your take on the problem. He or she will then help you delve a little deeper to see what other issues are intertwined and what repercussions are involved. Then you will embark upon a solution-finding process, much as you did in your divorce mediation. You will wind up with an agreement that details changes or modifications to your divorce agreement and may add new agreements or topics to it.

Then you are faced with the decision about whether you need to formalize the agreement with the court. In most instances it is best to do so, since it offers you legal protection and makes the agreement enforceable, such as for child support payments. But some couples see no reason to go through the expense and stress of filing court papers if all they've done is make some scheduling changes to a visitation agreement and their divorce decree gives them the authority to schedule times as they agree.

When mediating a dispute after divorce, be sure to:

163

• • •

- **Leave behind your old issues and disagreements.** You couldn't solve them before, so there's little chance you're going to be able to do so now.
- **Listen to what your ex is saying.** It's easy to think you know what someone means or needs, especially when you were once married to him or her. Space and time apart have probably changed both of you, so leave your assumptions at the door.
- **Try not to use mediation as a way to hold on to each other.** Remind yourself that you no longer belong to each other and you have less obligation to each other now than you did before. It can sometimes be tempting to use mediation as a way to have contact with each other.
- **Focus on your children's needs if you are mediating something to do with parenting.** Remember that your parenting plan was created to meet your children's needs, so these must come first.

Tips for Facing the Future

- Remember that you and your spouse may still have contact with each other and will need to use mediation skills to deal with problems that come up.
- Don't expect that you'll never need to see or speak to each other after the final papers come in the mail.
- If you have not already done so, develop rules that will govern your financial and personal dealings with each other.
- Remember that although you are divorced, you still have ties to each other and will need to work together to complete some tasks or to raise your children together.

◀12▶

Variations on a Theme

Mediation in Other Family Situations

Rae and Jack lived together and had a two-year-old son. They had never married. Their relationship was over, and it wasn't as simple as one of them just moving out. They had joint bank accounts, owned a home together, used each other's credit cards, and both wanted to spend time with their son. They did not understand what their rights were or if a court could even help them with their financial decisions. Rae read a magazine article about mediation and thought it could work for them. She got Jack's best friend to suggest it to him, and they found a mediator who helped them successfully work through the issues. They created a legal custody and child support agreement as well as a binding agreement about how they would divide their assets and debts.

Although family mediation is often thought of as being used in a divorce, it is suited for a variety of family problems, including couples who encounter problems after a divorce or life partners who were never married and share property or debts and/or have children together and need a way to resolve those issues when they split up. It is also an efficient process for people who have children together but were never a committed couple.

Mediation for the First Time After Divorce

If you are new to mediation but decide to try it to resolve some problems after your divorce, the process will certainly seem foreign to you. Read some of the earlier chapters for information about finding a mediator (Chapter 3) and understanding the process (Chapter 5). There are no required things you must decide—mediation is there to help you work out whatever problems you're encountering.

Mediation for Life Partners

If you and your partner (either opposite sex or same sex) are not formally married yet shared a life, commingling assets and debts or parenting children together, you are still essentially dissolving a marriage. Your mediator will take you through the normal divorce mediation process. The only difference is that there will be no laws that apply to many parts of your situation, though there may be previous cases that can offer guidance. If together you are legal parents of a child, your state's laws about custody, visitation, and child support will apply whether you are married or not. See Chapters 6 and 7 to guide you through these decisions.

Mediation gives you flexibility to negotiate things a court would not deal with. For example, if one of you is the legal parent of a child, but the other has not adopted the child, a court would not provide a visitation plan, since the nonparent has no legal rights to the child, despite the fact that he or she might have a deep and important relationship with the child. In mediation you are free to discuss the possibilities and come to a nonlegal agreement about continuing to make that person a part of the child's life.

The length of mediation will depend on the number of issues you have to decide. When you complete mediation you will have an agreement that contains all of your decisions. If you share legal

> ▶ *Words That Work* **Mediation for Unmarried**
> **Couples**
>
> Try these suggestions for talking to an unmarried partner about
> mediation:
>
> - We have to face the fact that we have a lot of things to decide.
>   Even if we don't have a piece of paper that says we're married,
>   we have to decide most of the things a married couple would.
> - We could go to court and get custody decided for us, but
>   wouldn't it be better if you and I could work something out
>   ourselves without a judge deciding?
> - We both bought many of the things in this house, and in
>   mediation we can work out a fair way to divide them.
> - I know you need help paying the rent for the first few months
>   after you move out; mediation could help us work through this.
> - I want you to be a part of my son's life, and I know you want
>   that, too, so let's go to mediation and figure out a way to make
>   it work.

parentage of children, a custody and child support agreement will
need to be filed with the court by your attorneys. The rest of your
agreement will not be filed with the court, but it is a contract, and
many parts can be enforced in court should one of you not honor
it. It is essential that you have your attorneys review your agreement before you sign it, whether or not it is going to court.

Mediation with a Parent Who Was Not Your Partner

If you have a child with another person and you have never lived
together and need to resolve issues of custody and child support,
mediation can be an excellent environment in which to do so. You
may know the other parent well, and if so, mediation will allow

you to continue to treat each other with mutual respect, while creating an agreement allowing your child access to both parents.

If you and the other do not know each other at all, mediation is also an excellent choice for you. Because you have no strong connection to each other, you don't know what to expect from each other, and there might be a lot of distrust and suspicion between you. Mediation can help you come to understand each other and your intentions and help you reach an agreement that will be fair to both of you.

Mediation with a New Partner

If you find a new partner and decide you want to live together or marry, you might use mediation to help you draw up a premarital agreement or to negotiate a cohabitation agreement. Your mediator can help you consider situations and problems you might not otherwise discuss in advance and can help you avoid a lot of common relationship problems down the road. Choose a mediator who is experienced in creating this kind of agreement and is comfortable working with couples in your situation.

Tips for Mediating Other Family Situations

When you mediate other family issues, look for a mediator who:

- Has experience working with couples in your situation.
- Has respect for your relationship and does not see it as inferior to "real" marriages.
- Has a clear concept of how to go about dealing with the issues you are facing.
- Has an understanding of the laws and case law that apply to your situation.
- Can recommend attorneys who have worked with couples in similar situations.

Appendix A

Sample Agreement to Mediate

Purpose of Mediation

The purpose of mediation is to help you resolve the issues between you. Mediation provides a forum where an impartial mediator will lead you in a cooperative problem-solving process so you can reach informed decisions on the matters that concern you. The understandings you reach will be included in your separation agreement or memorandum of understanding prepared by the mediator.

You agree that you are in mediation to decide separation or divorce issues and that the mediator will help you discuss and determine the best arrangements for you and your family regarding parenting, income needs, and all of the other arrangements needed for your separation or divorce.

Role of Mediator

The role of the mediator is to facilitate your communication, help you understand the decisions to be made, assist you in your discussion of the issues, and, as needed, help you generate alternatives to consider. *All* decisions are yours, and no settlement will be imposed upon you. It is understood that the mediator has no power or authority to decide issues for you. The parties understand that mediation is not a substitute for independent legal advice. You understand that the mediator cannot offer individual legal advice to either or both of you and will not provide therapy or arbitration. You understand that the mediator must remain completely impartial during the mediation process.

Role of Attorney and Advisors

The mediator recommends that you each consult separate attorneys to obtain legal advice regarding your rights and obligations. Upon written request from both spouses, the mediator will discuss with your attorneys any matters involved in the mediation. Consultation with other advisors, such as accountants, financial planners, tax experts, or appraisers, may also become necessary during the mediation and will be recommended to you when it seems appropriate. The actual selection of such advisors and payment of their fees will be made by you.

Voluntary Nature of Mediation

Mediation is a voluntary process, and no agreement or resolution will be forced upon you. Either of you is free to terminate the process at any time, as is the mediator. You both agree that you will not initiate or pursue divorce, separation, custody, child support, or other related matters in court while this mediation is ongoing.

Disclosure

In order for you to make fair decisions, honest and full disclosure of the family's financial situation (including assets and debts) and all other factors pertinent to the issues is necessary. You will be asked to complete financial disclosure forms and to provide copies of your income tax returns for the prior three years. It is also necessary that during the process no transfer or disposition of any property or securities be made and no debts be incurred by either of you without full disclosure to and agreement by the other.

Communication Guidelines

The most productive atmosphere for mediation is created when each person shows respect for the opinions and attitudes of the other even if there is disagreement between them. Each of you must refrain from telling the other what he or she needs, wants, or thinks. You must also try to listen to the other and to present your statements in the most effective way to have them heard and understood by the other. Name-calling, insults, and disparaging the other's opinions or requests does not encourage another to listen to you, and the mediator will help you avoid that.

Confidentiality

Certain financial documents you furnish may be submitted to the court and to your attorneys. Other than this, all information and records presented in the mediation are regarded as confidential by the mediator, and it is expected that you will do so as well. By signing this Agreement to Mediate, you agree not to subpoena or otherwise involve the mediator or any office staff or any records of this mediation in any court proceeding or lawsuit whatsoever. Mediation discussions and any drafts or unsigned agreements will not be admissible in any court or contested proceeding. You agree that the mediator may have caucus meetings with you individually and that all meetings and discussions will be confidential.

Fees

Fees for mediation sessions are $_____ per hour and are payable at the end of each session. Both parties are legally responsible for the payment of these fees. You may work out any arrangement between yourselves as to how you will divide the cost. In addition, a deposit of $_____ is required at the first mediation session, which will be applied to time spent outside the mediation session drafting your separation agreement or performing other necessary work on your behalf, such as having conversations with your attorneys or other advisors, which will be charged at the regular hourly rate. Any unused portion of the deposit will be refunded upon conclusion or termination of the mediation.

AGREEMENT TO MEDIATE

I agree to participate in the mediation process on the basis of the summary included herein, which I have read and discussed with the mediator. I understand that the mediator is providing a forum for mediation and discussion and that he/she is not offering legal advice or psychological counseling. I also affirm that I have been advised to consult with my own attorney, so as to be adequately advised about my legal rights and responsibilities regarding the issues being mediated.

I understand that I hereby waive any right of action that I may have against the mediator or his/her staff for any allegation of wrongdoing, absent gross negligence. I affirm, under penalty of damages, that I will not call upon the mediator or any member of his/her staff to act as a witness on my behalf in any court of record to testify to facts or conversations relating to any alleged deeds, wrongful acts, omissions, or commissions of the parties associated with this mediation.

I further affirm that I will not seek the production of notes or records of any mediation session that the mediator may have in his/her possession.

I understand the mediation fees are $_____ per hour for time spent on my behalf, both in and outside of the mediation sessions, and I agree to pay in full for all services rendered.

_____ (printed name)

_____

Signature of party   date

_____ (printed name)

_____

Signature of party   date

_____ (printed name)

_____

Signature of mediator   date

Appendix B

Resources

Organizations

American Academy of Matrimonial Lawyers
150 N. Michigan Avenue, Suite 2040
Chicago, IL 60601
312-263-6477
www.aaml.org

American Arbitration Association
335 Madison Avenue, 10th Floor
New York, NY 10017
212-716-5800
www.adr.org

American Association for Marriage and Family Therapy
112 S. Aldred Street
Alexandria, VA 22314
703-838-9808
www.aamft.org

American Bar Association, Section of Dispute Resolution
740 15th Street, NW
Washington, DC 20005
202-662-1680
www.abanet.org/dispute

American Bar Association, Section of Family Law
321 N. Clark Street
Chicago, IL 60610
312-988-5145
www.abanet.org/family/home.html

American Counseling Association
5999 Stevenson Avenue
Alexandria, VA 22304
800-347-6647
www.counseling.org

American Psychological Association
750 First Street, NE
Washington, DC 20002
800-374-2721
www.apa.org

Association for Conflict Resolution
1015 18th Street, NW, Suite 1150
Washington, DC 20036
202-464-9700
www.acrnet.org

Association of Attorney-Mediators
PO Box 741955
Dallas, TX 75374
800-280-1368
www.attorney-mediators.org

Association of Family and Conciliation Courts
6515 Grand Teton Plaza, Suite 210
Madison, WI 53719
608-664-3750
www.afccnet.org

Association of Independent Mediators
300 N. Michigan Avenue
South Bend, IN 46601
219-288-5100

Banana Splits (children's divorce support)
53 Columbus Avenue, #2
New York, NY 10023
212-262-4562

Children's Rights Council
6200 Editors Park Drive, Suite 103
Hyattsville, MD 20782
301-559-3120
www.gocrc.org

Coalition for Collaborative Divorce
PMB 623
23679 Calabasas
Calabasas, CA 91302
800-559-3724
www.nocourtdivorce.com

177
• • •

Equality in Marriage Institute
250 W. 57th Street, Suite 2404
New York, NY 10107
212-489-5590
www.equalityinmarriage.org

International Academy of Collaborative Professionals
c/o Paula Jackson
145 Wildhorse Valley Road
Novato, CA 94947
www.collabgroup.com

National Association for Community Mediation
1527 New Hampshire Avenue, NW
Washington, DC 20036
202-667-9700
www.nafcm.org

National Family Resiliency Center
2000 Century Plaza, Suite 121
Columbia, MD 21044
410-740-9553
www.divorceabc.com

Parents Without Partners
1650 Dixie Highway, Suite 510
Boca Raton, FL 33432
561-391-8833
www.parentswithoutpartners.org

State and Local Mediation Associations

Alabama

Alabama Center for Dispute Resolution
PO Box 671
Montgomery, AL 36101
334-269-0409
http://alabamaadr.org

Alaska

Alaska Dispute Settlement Association
PO Box 242922
Anchorage, AK 99524
907-258-0624
www.adsa.ws

Arizona

Superior Court of Arizona Alternative Dispute Resolution Program
www.superiorcourt.maricopa.gov/adr/index.asp

Arkansas

Arkansas Conflict Resolution Association
2024 Arkansas Valley Drive, Suite 305
Little Rock, AR 72212
501-224-0099

Arkansas Judiciary Alternative Dispute Resolution Commission
625 Marshall Street
Justice Building
Little Rock, AR 72201
501-682-9400
http://courts.state.ar.us/courts/adr.html

California

Association for Dispute Resolution of Northern California
601 Van Ness Avenue
San Francisco, CA 94102
650-745-3842
www.adrnc.org

California Association of Legal Mediators
PO Box 161321
Sacramento, CA 95816
916-444-2295

California Bar Association, Family Law Section, ADR South Committee
1925 Century Park East, Suite 2000
Los Angeles, CA 90067
310-277-2236

California Courts Family Court Services Programs
www.courtinfo.ca.gov/selfhelp/family/custody/programs.htm

California Dispute Resolution Council
PO Box 55020
Los Angeles, CA 90055
213-896-6540
www.cdrc.net

Northern California Mediation Center
Box 544
Corte Madera, CA 94976
415-927-4308
www.ncmc-mediate.org

Orange County Mediation and Investigative Services
www.occourts.org/juvenile/mediation.asp

Southern California Mediation Association
1405 Warner Avenue
Tustin, CA 92780
877-963-3428
www.scmediation.org

Colorado

Colorado Council of Mediators
3100 S. Sheridan Boulevard
Denver, CO 80227
800-864-4317
www.coloradomediation.org

Connecticut

Connecticut Council for Divorce Mediation and Family
Dispute Resolution
888-236-CCDM
www.ctmediators.org

Delaware

Delaware Federation for Dispute Resolution
PO Box 358
Wilmington, DE 19899
www.dfdr.org

Florida

Association of South Florida Mediators
224 SE 9th Street
Fort Lauderdale, FL 33316
954-524-8546
www.abcm.org

Florida Academy of Professional Mediators
800-808-8494
www.tfapm.org

Georgia
Family Mediation Association of Georgia
PO Box 2641
Decatur, GA 30031
404-373-4457

Georgia Commission on Dispute Resolution
404-463-3788
www.ganet.org/gadr

Georgia Council for Dispute Resolution
3350 Cumberland Circle, Suite LL75
Atlanta, GA 30339
800-866-0160

Hawaii
Hawaii State Judiciary Alternative Dispute Resolution Program
www.courts.state.hi.us/page_server/services/alternativedis
pute/4E3D896DFE782019EB28F79FE3.html

Idaho
Idaho Mediation Association
PO Box 2504
Boise, ID 83701
208-389-9211

Illinois
Mediation Association of Southern Illinois
PO Box 1833
Marion, IL 62959
618-453-3257
www.mediatenow.org

Mediation Council of Illinois
3540 N. Southport, #453
Chicago, IL 60657
312-641-3000
www.mediationcouncilofillinois.org

Indiana

Indiana Association of Mediators
6100 N. Keystone
Indianapolis, IN 46220
800-571-0260
www.mediation-indiana.org

Iowa

Iowa Association for Dispute Resolution
PO Box 3193
Iowa City, IA 52244
319-358-6690
www.iowaadr.org

Kansas

Heartland Mediators Association
8826 Santa Fe Drive, Suite 208
Overland Park, KS 66212
913-381-4458
www.heartlandmediators.org

Kentucky

Mediation Association of Kentucky
PO Box 1641
Frankfort, KY 40602
502-875-5633
www.kymediation.org

Louisiana
Family Mediation Council of Louisiana
888-658-9080
www.familymediationcouncil.com

Maine
Maine Association of Dispute Resolution Professionals
PO Box 8187
Portland, ME 04104
877-265-9712
www.madrp.org

Maine Judicial Branch Alternative Dispute Resolution
Program
www.courts.state.me.us/courtservices/adr/index.html

Maryland
Maryland Mediation and Conflict Resolution Office
900 Commerce Road
Annapolis, MD 21401
410-841-2260
www.courts.state.md.us/macro/index.html

Maryland Society of Professional Family Mediators
211 Massbury Street
Gaithersburg, MD 20878
301-947-0500
www.familymediator.com/society.html

Massachusetts
Massachusetts Association of Mediation
Practitioners and Programs
10133 Federal Street, 11th Floor
Boston, MA 02110
617-451-2093

Massachusetts Council on Family Mediation
23 Parker Road
Needham Heights, MA 02494
781-449-4430
www1.divorcenet.com/ma-mediators.html

Massachusetts Office of Dispute Resolution
617-727-2224
www.mass.gov/modr

New England Association for Conflict Resolution
1 Broadway, Suite 600
Cambridge, MA 02142
617-536-3227
www.neacr.org

Michigan

Michigan Council for Family and Divorce Mediation
489 Berrypatch Lane
White Lake, MI 48386
800-827-4390
www.familymediation.com

Minnesota

Minnesota Association of Custody Resolution Specialists
PO Box 1042
Willmar, MN 56201
320-732-4500

Conflict Resolution Minnesota
PO Box 11308
Minneapolis, MN 55411
612-879-4343
www.conflictresolutionmn.org

Mississippi

Mississippi Bar Alternative Dispute Resolution Section
PO Box 2168
Jackson, MS 39225
601-355-8635
www.msbar.org/mediators_directory_search.php or
www.msbar.org/7_alternative_dispute_resolution.php

Missouri

Association of Missouri Mediators
PO Box 67
Liberty, MO 64069
www.mediate.com/amm

Montana

Montana Mediation Association
PO Box 6363
Great Falls, MT 59406
406-727-8365
www.mtmediation.org

Nebraska

Mediation Association Network
8552 Cass Street
Omaha, NE 68114
402-397-0330

Nebraska Office of Dispute Resolution
521 S. 14th Street, Suite 200
Lincoln, NE 68509
402-471-3148
http://court.nol.org/odr

Nevada
Mediators of Southern Nevada
2470 S. Decatur Boulevard, Suite 110-M
Las Vegas, NV 89108
702-631-2790
www.mediatorsonv.com

New Hampshire
New Hampshire Alternative Dispute Resolution Program
www.courts.state.nh.us/adrp/index.htm

New Hampshire Conflict Resolution Association
PO Box 3263
Nashua, NH 03061
800-230-9903
www.nhcra.org

New Jersey
New Jersey Association of Professional Mediators
203 Towne Center Drive
Hillsborough, NJ 08844
800-981-4800
www.njapm.org

New Jersey Courts Statewide Mediation Program
www.judiciary.state.nj.us/services/medprogm.htm

New Mexico
New Mexico Center for Dispute Resolution
800 Park Avenue SW
Albuquerque, NM 87120
800-249-6884

New Mexico Mediation Association
PO Box 82384
Albuquerque, NM 87198
505-266-6560
http://nmma.info

New York

Family and Divorce Mediation Council of Greater New York
114 W. 47th Street, Suite 2200
New York, NY 10036
212-978-8590
www.divorcemediationny.org

Greater New York Association for Conflict Resolution
250 W. 57th Street, Suite 817
New York, NY 10107
212-946-1998
www.acrgny.org

Mediation Council of Central New York Family Mediation Center
7000 Genesee Street, Building B
Fayetteville, NY 13066
315-446-5513

New York State Council on Divorce Mediation
585 Stewart Avenue, Suite 610
Garden City, NY 11530
800-894-2646
www.nysmediate.org

New York State Dispute Resolution Association
255 River Street, 4th Floor
Troy, NY 12180
518-687-2240
www.nysdra.org

Rochester Association of Family Mediators
PO Box 10872
Rochester, NY 14610
585-234-2392
www.rafm.net

North Carolina
Mediation Network of North Carolina
4208 Six Forks Road
Raleigh, NC 27609
919-783-8483
www.mnnc.org

North Carolina Association of Professional Family Mediators
189 College Street
Asheville, NC 28801
704-251-6089
http://familymediators.org/index.html

North Carolina Dispute Resolution Commission
PO Box 2448
Raleigh, NC 27602
919-981-5077
www.nccourts.org/courts/crs/councils/drc/default.asp

North Dakota
North Dakota Alternative Dispute Resolution Program
www.court.state.nd.us/court/adr

Ohio

Ohio Mediation Associates
2897 Liberty Bell Lane
Reynoldsburg, OH 43068
937-264-2336
www.mediateohio.org

Supreme Court of Ohio Dispute Resolution Program
www.sconet.state.oh.us/dispute_resolution

Oklahoma

Oklahoma Academy of Mediators and Arbitrators
119 N. Robinson, Suite 1100
Oklahoma City, OK 73102
405-366-6100
www.oama.org

Oregon

Oregon Mediation Association
PO Box 2952
Portland, OR 97208
503-872-9775
www.mediate.com/oma

Pennsylvania

Family Mediation Association of the Delaware Valley
PO Box 15934
Philadelphia, PA 19103
215-545-4227

Pennsylvania Council of Mediators
www.pamediation.org

Rhode Island
Newport County Association of Mediators
580 Thames Street, Suite 207
Newport, RI 02840
888-873-6226

Rhode Island Judiciary Divorce Mediation
www.courts.state.ri.us/family/mediation.htm

South Carolina
Low Country Mediation Network
PO Box 1404
Charleston, SC 29402
803-727-6613

South Carolina Alternative Dispute Resolution Program
www.scbar.org/member/adr/default.asp

South Dakota
South Dakota Mediation Association
Dakota Hall 119-USD
414 E. Clark Street
Vermillion, SD 57069
www.usd.edu/sdma/main.html

Tennessee
Mediation Association of Tennessee
118 29th Avenue, S
PO Box 121541
Nashville, TN 37212
615-646-9363

Tennessee Alternative Dispute Resolution Program
www.tsc.state.tn.us/geninfo/programs/adr/adrdir.asp

Tennessee Mediators Network
807 W. First North Street
Morristown, TN 37814
www.tnmediators.com

Texas

Austin Association of Mediators
1409 W. 6th Street
Austin, TX 78703
512-476-7226
www.austinmediators.org

College of Texas Mediators
1821 Stonegate
Denton, TX 76205
972-221-9333

Family Mediation Network of Greater Houston
Memorial City Plaza
800 Gessner, Suite 252
Houston, TX 77024
713-465-2347

192

Texas Association of Mediators
PO Box 191208
Dallas, TX 75219
713-629-1416
www.txmediator.org

Texas State Bar Alternative Dispute Resolution Section
www.texasadr.org

Utah
Utah Association of Family Mediators
6914 S. 3000 East, #205
Salt Lake City, UT 84121
801-944-5400

Vermont
Vermont Family Court Mediation Program
www.vermontjudiciary.org/mediation/default.htm

Vermont Mediators Association
PO Box 1108
Montpelier, VT 05601
http://vma.freeyellow.com

Virginia
Central Virginia Mediation
3401 Brook Road
Richmond, VA 23233
804-646-3451
www.cvco.org/civic/organ/cvmednet

Virginia Alternative Dispute Resolution Program
www.courts.state.va.us/drs/main.htm

Virginia Mediation Network
2108 W. Laburnum Avenue, Suite 220
Richmond, VA 23227
804-254-2666
www.vamediation.org

Washington

Mediation Consortium of Washington State
1122 E. Pike Street, #1095
Seattle, WA 98122
206-833-3803

Washington State Dispute Resolution
Washington State Bar Association
2101 Fourth Avenue, 4th Floor
Seattle, WA 98121
www.adr-wa.com

West Virginia

West Virginia Family Court-Ordered Mediation
www.state.wv.us/wvsca/familyct/cover.htm

West Virginia Center for Dispute Resolution
PO Box 828
Morgantown, WV 26507
304-296-2124
www.wvcdr.org

West Virginia Parent Education and Mediation Project
205 E. King Street
Martinsburg, WV 25401
304-267-0038

Wisconsin

Wisconsin Association of Mediators
PO Box 44578
Madison, WI 53744
608-848-1970
www.wamediators.org

Websites

ADR Resources: http://adrr.com

American Academy of Matrimonial Lawyers referral program: www.aaml.org/directory.htm

American Bar Association lawyer referral services: www.abanet.org/legalservices/lris/directory.html

American Responsible Divorce Network: www.proactive -coach.com/divorce

Home appraisal information: http://appraiserusa.com

Association of Attorney-Mediators mediator locator: www.attorney-mediators.org/directory.html

Association of Divorce Financial Planners: www.divorceandfinance.com

Business evaluation information: www.bulletproofbizplans.com/BallPark

Car Blue Book value: www.kbb.com

Child support calculators by state: www.alllaw.com/calculators/childsupport

Choosing a child therapist: http://kidshealth.org/parent/ emotions/feelings/finding_therapist.html

Choosing a therapist: http://psychcentral.com/therapst.htm

Collaborative law: www.mediate.com/collaborativelaw

Conflict Resolution Information Source: www.crinfo.org

Divorce and Children: www.divorceandchildren.com

Divorce Interactive: www.divorceinteractive.com

Divorce Magazine: www.divorcemag.com

DivorceNet: www.divorcenet.com

Divorce Resource Center: www.divorce-resource-center.com

Mediate.com: www.mediate.com

Model standards of practice for family and divorce mediation: www.onlineresolution.com/om-standards.cfm

National Coalition Against Domestic Violence: www.ncadv.org

National Financial Planning Support Center's Find a CFP Professional: www.fpanet.org/plannersearch/ plannersearch.cfm

Realtor Finder: www.realtorfinder.com

Separation and divorce articles: www.yoursocialworker
.com/sep-dev.htm

State and local bar association directory: www.abanet
.org/barserv/stlobar.html

State divorce laws: www.findlaw.com

Therapist locator: www.aamft.org/therapistlocator/
index.asp

Woman's Divorce: www.womansdivorce.com

Books

Conscious Divorce: Ending a Marriage with Integrity by Susan
Allison (Three Rivers Press, 2001).

Crazy Time: Surviving Divorce and Building a New Life by Abi-
gail Trafford (Perennial, 1992).

Divorce and Money by Violet Woodhouse (Nolo, 2002).

*Divorce Is a Mitzvah: A Practical Guide to Finding Wholeness
and Holiness When Your Marriage Dies* by Perry Netter (Jew-
ish Lights Publishing, 2002).

The Divorce Organizer and Planner by Brette McWhorter Sember (McGraw-Hill, 2004).

Divorce: Six Ways to Get Through the Bad Times for Good by
Jack Williamson and Mary Ann Salerno (Bridge Builder
Media, 2001).

*The Divorced Dad's Survival Book: How to Stay Connected with
Your Kids* by David Knox (Perseus, 2000).

*Healthy Divorce: For Parents and Children—An Original Clini-
cally Proven Program for Working Through the Fourteen
Stages of Separation, Divorce, and Remarriage* by Craig
Everett and Sandra Volgy Everett (Jossey-Bass, 1998).

Helping Your Kids Cope with Divorce the Sandcastles Way by M. Gary Neuman (Random House, 1999).

How to Parent with Your Ex: Working Together for Your Child's Best Interest by Brette McWhorter Sember (Sourcebooks, 2005).

Not Your Mother's Divorce: A Practical, Girlfriend-to-Girlfriend Guide to Surviving the End of a Young Marriage by Kay Moffett and Sarah Touborg (Broadway, 2003).

100 Answers to Your Questions on Annulments by Edward Peters (Basilica Press, 1997).

Vicky Lansky's Divorce Book for Parents: Helping Your Children Cope with Divorce and Its Aftermath by Vicky Lansky (Book Peddlers, 1996).

We're Still Family: What Grown Children Have to Say About Their Parents' Divorce by Constance Ahrons (HarperCollins, 2004).

Your Divorce Advisor: A Lawyer and a Psychologist Guide You Through the Legal and Emotional Landscape of Divorce by Diana Mercer and Marsha Pruett (Fireside, 2001).

Helping Your Kids Cope with Divorce the Sandcastles Way by M. Gary Neuman (Random House, 1999).

How to Parent with Your Ex: Working Together for Your Child's Best Interest by Brette McWhorter Sember (Sourcebooks, 2005).

Not Your Mother's Divorce: A Practical, Girlfriend-to-Girlfriend Guide to Surviving the End of a Young Marriage by Kay Moffett and Sarah Touborg (Broadway, 2003).

100 Answers to Your Questions on Annulments by Edward Peters (Basilica Press, 1997).

Vicky Lansky's Divorce Book for Parents: Helping Your Children Cope with Divorce and Its Aftermath by Vicky Lansky (Book Peddlers, 1996).

We're Still Family: What Grown Children Have to Say About Their Parents' Divorce by Constance Ahrons (HarperCollins, 2004).

Your Divorce Advisor: A Lawyer and a Psychologist Guide You Through the Legal and Emotional Landscape of Divorce by Diana Mercer and Marsha Pruett (Fireside, 2001).

Index